THE JEWS AGAINST ROME

The Jews Against Rome

Susan Sorek

continuum

Continuum UK, The Tower Building, 11 York Road, London SE1 7NX
Continuum US, 80 Maiden Lane, Suite 704, New York, NY 10038

www.continuumbooks.com

First published 2008

British Library Cataloguing-in-Publication Data
A catalogue record for this book is available from the British Library.

ISBN 978 1 84725 248 7

Typeset by Pindar New Zealand

Printed and bound by MPG Books Ltd, Cornwall, Great Britain

Contents

To David Noy, friend, colleague and mentor.

Introduction

Scholars have concluded that in comparative terms the Jewish war, culminating in the siege of Jerusalem, and destruction of the Temple was *the* major event in Roman military history. The war demanded a massive concentration of forces and was the longest siege in the whole of the imperial period. Lasting roughly five months it took four legions, detachments of two others, 20 infantry cohorts, eight mounted *alae* and 18,000 men supplied by four independent kings to effect a victory. In fact the forces that were committed to the siege were larger than those deployed for the invasion of Britain in AD 43.

The revolt was not inspired by any ideological objection on the part of the Jews towards Rome, nor any Roman anti-Semitism. There were a variety of underlying causes that helped spark the revolt; social tensions, bad procurators, the divisions amongst the ruling class, the rise of banditry and poor harvests, but perhaps the most significant feature of all was the apocalyptical storm brewing over first-century Palestine.

Of all the messianic movements one in particular drew the most attention; the Essene sect, the community that wrote the Dead Sea Scrolls, based their calculations on the end of days on a prophecy from the book of Daniel. Josephus says that the major impetus inspiring the Jewish revolt against Roman rule was an 'oracle found in the sacred scriptures'. This oracle effectively said when the time came 'one from their own country would become ruler of the world'. The Essenes calculated the year AD 26/7 ushered in the messianic age. There was never a time previously quite like it, and there has never been one since; two messiahs, one king one priest would rule over Palestine. The fervour with which many fought against the might of the greatest power of the ancient world could only have come from such beliefs; that the end of days was nigh.

All revolutions change history, whether they are successful or not and the Jewish war against Rome in AD 66–70 is no exception. Even though the revolution did not succeed, the ramifications were enormous and still impact upon the modern-day world. The revolt had a profound influence on the development of Judaism and Christianity, to which modern times bear witness. Had this revolt not occurred, then two major religions would simply not exist, at least certainly not in their present form. The structures and theologies of these religions owe a great deal to the crisis provoked by the revolt and destruction of the Temple in

Jerusalem. For Judaism especially the destruction was an axial moment in the formation of rabbinic Judaism, enabling the Pharasaic sect to reorganize Judaism as a conformative religion. Christianity also emerged in its Pauline form, which attested Jesus to be, as one author has succinctly put it, 'repackaged as a saviour God dispensing opiate'.[1] By the late second century AD Christian writers saw the destruction of the Temple as definitive proof of God's desire that the Christian church was to be the successor of the 'old religion', and its doctrines to constitute the *New Israel*.

The other exceptional fact about the Jewish war is the extraordinary amount of information to have survived and for that we have to thank one man, Flavius Josephus, a Jew of Pharisaic origin and eyewitness to the events he describes. Born Joseph ben Mattiyahu, of aristocratic descent he played a key role in many of the events during the conflict with Rome. He held a command in Galilee during a pivotal stage of the revolt, was captured by the Romans, and eventually through his skilful manipulation of events became a client and friend to the future Roman emperors, Vespasian and his son Titus, working as a translator and mediator during the fateful siege of Jerusalem: to the Jews he became a traitor. He left his native Judaea with the Roman forces, never to return but to spend the remainder of his life as a Roman citizen in Rome changing his name to Flavius Josephus, writing accounts both for himself and for his Roman masters on the Jewish war.[2] In his works *Jewish War* (referred to hereafter as *JW*), *Life* and *Jewish Antiquities* (*JA*) he pursues a number of questions and agendas; as writer and historian he is both defender of Jewish traditions and the Jewish people to a predominately Roman audience. He often depicts the people of Judaea and Galilee as noble, fervent in their commitment to God and generally good citizens.[3]

However the veracity of his work is often called into question because of the discrepancies in his accounts of the same events in *JW* and *Life*. Many scholars argue these occur because of the pressures he was subjected to during the 30 years he lived and wrote in Rome.[4]

On the other hand some have attempted to play down the discrepancies, and one in particular has argued that it is ill-founded to use Josephus as a completely reliable historical source because he was, for personal reasons, intent on explaining the most important events in his life which occurred between AD 66–70. In doing so he searched the annals of his society to find the causes for the disaster. From his perspective it would appear there had to be some explanation, whereas from a modern perspective we could conclude there was nothing inevitable about what happened, that it was just an accident.[5] However each attack upon Josephus' history undermines the study of the subject altogether. Yet others have proposed that the rich, mostly priestly Judaean elite's involvement in the revolt was an important factor in 'encouraging Rome to treat the uprising as a full scale rebellion and provoking the splits that plagued the short lived independent Judaean state'.[6] Seemingly the Judaean ruling class was driven into revolution because they were unable to control pressures, mainly economic, from the rest of Judaean society.

The revolutionary zeal the revolt had inspired did not entirely die out; there were still pockets of resistance in many corners of the Roman Empire. Some Zealots escaped to Alexandria in Egypt where they attempted to create a new base of operations. They were rounded up by the citizens and handed over to the Romans. The old zeal was still apparent as the captives continued to defy the Romans even under torture. At Cyrene another revolutionary, Jonathan, a weaver by trade, led a number of poorer citizens out into the desert promising to show them signs and portents. Once again a military force was sent to capture them, Jonathan was hunted down and taken to Rome where he was tortured and burnt alive.

There were further disturbances between the years AD 115–117 in the cities of the Diaspora, in Cyrene, Egypt and Cyprus and finally once again in Palestine. The new Jewish messiah Simon bar Kochba (Son of the Star), supported by the greatest sage of the time, the radical Rabbi Akiva, rose up against Roman occupation. The rebels seized back the Holy city of Jerusalem, appointed a new High Priest and restored Temple ritual. Many exiles now returned to Palestine, and the countryside was once again home to guerrilla bands, the caves and desert fortresses played host to rebel defenders. This time it took the Romans four years and eight legions to crush the revolt. Sadly the details of this rebellion are scant, unlike the earlier Jewish war, whose story is contained in this work, following the accounts of its *star witness* Josephus.

Where there is some disparity in his work an attempt has been made to shed some light on the possible reasons for this, using modern scholarly research. Nevertheless there is still much that is not precise, even the archaeological record cannot fill the gaps in knowledge. Recent excavations of some of the sites mentioned in the text are discussed in Chapter 15 and show in some instances Josephus' words are true, but the final judgement concerning the causes and consequences of the war must be left to the reader. What is true is that the war against Rome was an axial moment in Jewish history, and in consequence for the history of the Western world.

The Historical Background: 198 BC–AD 66

In 198 BC Antiochus II of Syria (Seleucid dynasty, named after its founder, one of Alexander the Great's generals) finally won control of Palestine from Ptolemy V of Egypt. Ten years later his victorious armies were confronted by the Roman legions at Magnesia, in Asia Minor. Their defeat and the harsh peace dictated by Rome, the rising power in the Mediterranean, shook the Seleucid dynasty to its foundations. During the next three reigns of the Seleucid kings, a second confrontation with Rome was feared. In order to combat this threat a spirit of unity in the heterogeneous kingdom needed to be fostered, and that could only be achieved through an appeal to the religious tenets of Hellenic society.

Under Seleucid rule the cities had complete autonomy in all internal affairs, the only limitations on their liberty were the supervision of a royal official, and to conform to the king's policy on all external issues. The Seleucids had always been zealous Hellenizers in their many dominions; King Antiochus IV, who adopted the title Epiphanes (God manifest), had two aims, to religiously unify his kingdom by instituting the worship of Olympian Zeus, and to unify the Hellenistic world by conquering Egypt and supplanting the Ptolemaic dynasty with his own.

Palestine came under Seleucid control for almost two centuries and during their rule Hellenization in the country advanced rapidly bringing with it all the amenities of Greek life, especially athletics, which attracted many of the younger elements including some of the younger priests. There had always been tension between the conservative High Priests and those who promoted the more worldly Hellenistic values. The Hellenizers managed to persuade Antiochus IV to remove the High Priest Onias IV, and appoint his brother Jason, but some of the more extreme elements of this faction were not satisfied and tried to depose Jason and replaced him with one of their own group, a man named Menelaus, whose qualifications for the role were questionable to say the least. He managed to persuade the king and his advisers that the Jewish nation was willing to adopt Greek culture and beliefs. However, while Antiochus was in Egypt the deposed Jason made an attempt to take Jerusalem. This gave Antiochus the excuse he needed to send in his troops and once the city was taken the process of his 'religious unification' began. The Temple treasures were appropriated, the sacred precincts turned over to the cult of Zeus and Dionysus-Sabazios, and the altar defiled by sacrificing swine on it. The Hellenizers built a separate city on the western hill opposite the Temple and set up a polis with the intention of naming it 'Antioch in Jerusalem'. A fortress was constructed called the Acra, which faced and partly commanded the Temple and contained a garrison of royal troops.

However, it soon became apparent that Menelaus had deceived Antiochus, for the Jews had no desire to accept Greek gods and a Greek altar set up in the Temple, and offered strong resistance. At first the extremists amongst the Hellenizers tried to wipe out this resistance, the practice of Judaism was forbidden and the Jews ordered to make sacrifices to the alien gods. Many Jews fled the city, but many remained and defied the order; consequently they were put to death. This was the first religious persecution in recorded history and open rebellion soon followed.

The Maccabean rebellion against Antiochus began not in Jerusalem but in the town of Modein, which belonged to the toparchy of Lydda, which lay adjacent to Judaea. When the king's officials arrived there to 'compel the men to sacrifice', Mathathias the Hasmonean, a resident priest, killed the attendant apostate and the king's officer proclaiming that 'if all the nations that are in the house of the King's domain hearken unto him … yet and I and my sons will walk in the covenant of our fathers'.[1] Mathathias together with his five sons fled into the hills and from there conducted a guerrilla war, tearing down heathen altars and pursuing, as they referred to them *the sons of pride*, the Hellenizing Jews. They were soon joined by a company of Hasidaeans, a group of pious men who were now ready to fight for the faith. Shortly afterwards Mathathias died and his third son, Judas Maccabaeus, who was a natural strategic genius, took his place as leader. Under his leadership the rebels soon overran the whole of Judaea, cutting off the Syrian garrison and its supporters in Jerusalem.

The king mounted four operations to relieve the blockade of Jerusalem. The first attempt failed, so a second attempt was made under the command of Apollonius, governor of Samaria, to whom Judaea was administratively subject; this too resulted in failure when Apollonius was routed and slain in the ascent of Lebonah. This alarmed Seron, commander of the royal forces of Coele-Syria under which Samaria came; he marched down through Beth Horon but was defeated in a surprise ambush by Judas. However, by this time Antiochus had decided to assert his authority in Persia; before setting out he nominated his kinsman Lysias as regent of the lands west of the Euphrates. Lysias assembled an army with Ptolemy, Nicanor and Gorgias as generals. They set up camp near Emmaus at the foot of the mountains that surrounded Jerusalem. Judas and his rebel army took up position half way between Jerusalem and the enemy so when the generals decided to split their forces and send them into the hills Judas readily took advantage and attacked the troops left at Emmaus, capturing the camp and pursuing the enemy as far as the royal fortress at Gezer. He then returned to face the rest of the enemy but Gorgias declined battle and made a hasty withdrawal.

Lysias now took the field and arrived at the borders of Judaea from the south confronting Judas at Beth-zur. The details of what actually happened are fragmentary but apparently Lysias was pushed back and Judas was free to march into Jerusalem and take possession of the Temple. The shrine was cleansed and sacrifices were resumed. The day, 25th of Kislev 165 BC and the following seven days, are still commemorated by Jews all over the world as the Feast of Dedication or 'Chanukah'.

Judas, with the help of his brother Simon, then undertook the rescue of the Jews of western Galilee who were being oppressed by the Gentiles. The Jews of Gilead were evacuated to Jerusalem, and many Jews living in Galilee were brought to Judaea. Judas had successes over his enemies east of the Jordan and Idumaea, and wreaked vengeance on the people of Jaffa for their treatment of the Jews there, issuing a similar threat to the people of Jamnia.

Meanwhile Antiochus IV died while on campaign in Persia and his young son Antiochus V Eupator was proclaimed king. In order to establish Seleucid supremacy another campaign was launched against Judaea. As before the armies clashed at Beth-zur, this time Judas was forced to withdraw and retired to Gophna. The young king and his regent succeeded in taking Jerusalem and destroyed the Temple fortifications. Eljakim (Alkimos) was appointed High Priest, and managed to win the support of the Hasidaeans who recognized him as a descendant of Aaron, *the man of peace*. The Syrian general Nicanor was stationed in Jerusalem to enforce the new regime.

Nevertheless, Judas and his supporters continued the struggle for an independent nation believing religious freedom could only be achieved in this way. Ironically, they were assisted in their efforts by Rome, who were looking for ways in which to undermine the Seleucids who they regarded as the strongest of the Greek states in the east. They made an alliance with Judas, and took up the Jewish cause.

However, the Seleucid dynasty was showing signs of internal division. Antiochus IV had superseded his nephew Demetrius, the son of his elder brother Seleucus IV. Demetrius who believed he had more of a legitimate claim to the throne came to Antioch and deposed Antiochus V. This marked the beginning of the end for the Seleucid dynasty; from this point onwards the struggle for power between their descendants gradually eroded the Seleucid Empire.

Judas managed to defeat Nicanor in battle, but Demetrius dispatched his general Bacchides to Judaea and Judas was killed in the battle at Eleasa. His death was mourned by the whole nation who now found themselves in great peril. Those rebels that had survived the battle chose the youngest son of Mathathias, Jonathan, to be their leader; he decided they should withdraw to the Judaean wilderness, where they managed to hold out for three years. The

Syrian commander fortified Judaea with a series of linked citadels, but Jonathan managed to gain a foothold in the area at Beth-basi near Bethlehem. Finally the divisions within the Seleucid dynasty had led to a mounting crisis and Bacchides was forced to withdraw his forces from Judaea. Jonathan was able to settle at Michmash as 'de facto' ruler of Judaea (with the exception of Jerusalem and Beth-zur). Finally in 152 BC he obtained permission from Demetrius I to transfer his seat to Jerusalem and was nominated High Priest by Demetrius' rival Alexander Balas, another pretender to the throne, who claimed to be the son of Antiochus Epiphanes and therefore legitimate heir.

For ten years Jonathan was caught up in Seleucid power politics, he often backed the weaker of the pretenders to the throne; he enlarged his kingdom and built up a substantial army, which at the battle of Jamnia in 147 BC proved to be one of the strongest armies south of Seleucid dominions. He became Lord of the old province of Judaea, supplemented by the districts of Lydda, Arimathaea and Apharaima by Accaron and other lands beyond the Jordan. He was treacherously executed by the Syrian general Tryphon, and was succeeded by Simon, the last of the five Hasmonean brothers.

Simon managed to raze the Acra in 143 BC, so finally delivering Jerusalem from its foreign oppressor. He also managed to annexe Jaffa enabling Judaea to have access to the Mediterranean Sea. He took Gezer and made a secure road to Jerusalem and finally in 141 BC was granted independence from Seleucid rule obtaining the right to mint coinage. Simon was assassinated in 135 BC by his son-in-law, and succeeded by his son John Hyrcanus I. Shortly after the accession of Hyrcanus I Judaea was attacked once more by Antiochus VI Sidetes, and after another siege of the city that lasted for a year, Antiochus was able to impose his terms, which were the return of Jaffa and Gezer to Seleucid authority, and breaching of the walls of Jerusalem.

The victory was, however, short-lived for when Antiochus VI died in 129 BC, John Hyrcanus I quickly resumed his conquests. The majority of the Greek cities along the interior were already free from Seleucid rule so John began his campaigns in the mountainous areas of Judaea and Samaria. The first cities to fall were Medeba and Heshbon beyond the River Jordan; with these cities under his control he now straddled the international trade route from Damascus to the Red Sea. He then turned his attention towards the Samaritans, whom he subdued (although they kept their own character under the Hasmoneans). In south Judaea the Idumaeans were obliged to adopt Judaism, and it became fixed policy throughout the rest of Hasmonean rule to attach new areas to Judaea through religious links. In the north of the country the city of Samaria came under attack, and after a long siege John overran the Beth-Shean Valley and the inner Carmel region.

However, towards the end of his reign there was an internal rift. The Pharisees, who had succeeded the Hasidaeans, the priests who had fought alongside Judas Maccabaeus, became disturbed by the increasing amount of Hellenization taking place. For John and his followers this had been a necessary evil, something not readily understood by the masses; these differences of opinion would in the coming years escalate bringing about the destruction of the newly won independence.

John died in 104 BC, and was succeeded by his son Judah I Aristobulus, who reigned for one year. In that year Galilee was taken from the Ituraeans and soon after its annexation became wholly Jewish. The next Hasmonean king was Alexander Jannaeus, another son of Jonathan. In contrast to Judah he had a long reign (103–76 BC), under his rule Palestine was almost completely unified for the first time since the reign of King David. In a series of expeditions to the south-west and east, the north-west and east, the Jewish independent state was extended and included the Carmel and its coast, the Jordan Valley up to Dan and Paneas, and nearly all of the Transjordan Mountains. Jannaeus occupied the northern bank of the Dead Sea making it a domestic lake of Judaea; took Gaza and lands as far as the River of Egypt (Wadi el-Arish).

Jannaeus fought many battles but surprisingly never won one: after every defeat he resumed the struggle until he eventually vanquished his enemy and to aid him he used Greek mercenaries. His maritime policy also amounted to little more than piracy. The Greek cities were given the option of adopting Judaism or leaving their city; the archaeological record shows that presumably Jews later resettled many of the deserted cities.

His internal policy presented even more difficulties, it seems he alienated the Pharisees by his assumption of the trappings of kingship, which implied the abolition of the constitutional cooperation between prince and *heber* (the council of elders who represented the people). His adversaries rose up in insurrection and called on the Seleucid king; the outcome was a battle between Jewish rebels allied with the Syrian army versus the Greek mercenaries of a Jewish monarch. Jannaeus eventually won, and succeeded in reconciling most of his people. He died in the field of battle besieging the town of Ragba, east of Jordan: on his deathbed he asked his Queen and successor, Salome Alexandra to make peace with the Pharisees.

With his death the Hasmonean dynasty came to end. Although the Hasmoneans had saved the Jewish nation from extinction, they failed to reconcile the conflict between Greek culture and the spiritual needs of the Jews, an issue that would have disastrous results in the ensuing crisis that was looming in the east.

The end of Seleucid rule brought in its wake a period of general anarchy throughout the east. Some oriental rulers, for example Tigranes I of Armenia and Mithridates VI of Pontus continued their endeavour to establish oriental rule throughout the Hellenistic world. By this time the Romans were firmly entrenched in the east, having established the province of Asia in 133 BC. Their rule was not well received because of the general greed and oppression displayed by their governors and merchants, so the Greeks of Asia joined forces with Mithridates in his war against Rome in 88 BC. However, Rome was also struggling with internal conflicts, the social and political upheavals that would herald the fall of the Republic. Nevertheless Rome prevailed and repelled Mithridates' assault in Greece; they also vanquished his allies, the pirates of Cilicia and Crete. But in the second Mithridatic war (83–81 BC) Mithridates was successful. In a third conflict with Rome in 74 BC he obtained the services of Roman officers of the Marian faction (those who allied themselves to Marius the Roman general who marched against Rome in 86 BC after the civil war with Sulla), and at first prospered but he was persuaded to take refuge with Tigranes I of Armenia and both were beaten. In 66 BC Pompey the Great, the general and future protagonist of Julius Caesar, defeated him on the Euphrates and Mithridates was forced to flee to the Crimea, where he finally took his own life.

Tigranes had by 74 BC managed to extend his authority as far as Acre, but he also saw his capital destroyed. In 64 BC the army of Pompey the Great entered Antioch, and Rome became in effect master of the eastern Mediterranean. One of the consequences of Pompey's victory was the reduction of Syria to a Roman province. All the rulers who had divided the Seleucid territories amongst themselves now faced the threat of the might of Rome.

The Jews were perhaps the least well equipped to deal with this threat. The reign of Queen Alexandra (76–67 BC) was spent in a succession of quarrels between the Pharisees who now held power, and Alexandra's kinsmen. This conflict was personified in the rivalry between John Hyrcanus II, who succeeded his father as High Priest and Jannaeus' younger son, Judah Aristobulus II, who represented the Sadducees (the elitist group from whom many High Priests were selected), who were antagonistic to the Pharisees. When Hyrcanus II succeeded Queen Alexandra civil war broke out. Aristobulus forced his brother to abdicate, so Hyrcanus found the Idumaean, Antipater (a member of the Hasmonaean dynasty) a ready ally, together they fled to the Nabataen king Aretas, who agreed to help Hyrcanus on condition all the conquests made by Jannaeus south-east of the Dead Sea would be returned to the Nabataeans. While the army of Hyrcanus and Aretas were besieging Jerusalem the Roman general Scaurus arrived with orders from Pompey to put an end to the fighting. They withdrew to Philadelphia and here Aristobulus routed them at a place called Papyron, near the Jordan.

It was at this juncture Roman intervention in Judaean affairs took a decisive turn. Pompey summoned the brothers to Damascus and after listening to their arguments decided in favour of the weaker Hyrcanus. Aristobulus tried to resist the decision and was captured by the advancing Roman army at Alexandrium, in the Jordan Valley. Despite this setback his supporters continued their resistance on Temple Mount: finally in 63 BC the Roman legions stormed the sanctuary.

Pompey had two aims in Judaea; the first was to establish Roman supremacy and the second to reinforce Hellenism by revitalizing the Greek cities. However, Rome had no rigid policy when it came to dealing with subjugated nations. Syria was annexed, the Nabataeans, whose territory was remote and difficult to occupy, lost Damascus but were allowed to retain the remainder of the territory; the Ituraeans had to relinquish their coastal cities, but were given more domains in the Bashan; the Jews however were harshly dealt with. They were allowed to keep only Judaea and eastern Idumaea, Galilee and Jewish Peraea east of Jordan: all the cities taken by Hyrcanus and Jannaeus regained their former status. Pompey, in order to make the cities east of Jordan better able to defend themselves joined them, together with Scythopolis, into a League of Ten Cities (Decapolis). Hyrcanus, together with his minister Antipater II, was left to rule the rest of the Jewish territory.

The Greek cities on the coastal plain and east of the Jordan were restored, but those inland took a little longer, only Samaria and Scythopolis were re-established. Pompey's successor was Gabinius and he was plagued by revolts from Aristobulus and his son Alexander, which took him three long campaigns to suppress. He tried unsuccessfully to split Judaea into five separate regions, Jerusalem, Jericho, Ammathus, Adoraim and Sepphoris, each to be governed by its own Sanhedrin (council).

In Rome the civil war that ensued between Pompey and Julius Caesar resulted in Antipater aiding Caesar in his campaign in Alexandria, Egypt. The victorious Caesar elevated Hyrcanus to the rank of Ethnarch, and Antipater was made Administrator General (Epitropos) of Judaea. Caesar also returned Jaffa and the Jezreel Valley to the Jews but ignored the pleas of Aristobulus' sons to reinstate them. Antipater appointed his sons Phasael and Herodes (Herod) as governors of Jerusalem and Galilee, and after his assassination in 42 BC they continued to rule under Roman protection. Herod was ruthless; his illegal slaughter of Galilean rebels brought him before the Sanhedrin in Jerusalem for trial, but he managed to defy his judges and went unpunished.

Pompey's settlement lasted until the assassination of Julius Caesar in 44 BC. The anarchic period that followed saw a number of vying Roman factions ruling in the east. First the Republicans, then the triumvirs Antony and Octavian (later the emperor Augustus), finally Antony and Cleopatra, all had one aim, money and power. Amid all the confusion the Hasmonaean party and the ambitious Idumaeans both saw opportunities to advance themselves. Mathathias Antigonus the surviving son of Aristobulus II tried to attack Herod in 43 BC but lost the battle. Mark Antony appointed Phasael and Herod as tetrarchs under Hyrcanus, which virtually gave them control of the whole of Judaea.

The greatest threat to Rome at this time came from their old enemies Parthia

(Persia); the Parthians launched an attack invading Syria and Judaea in 40 BC, and were joined by a band of Jews from the Carmel and the Drymos forest in the Sharon. Phasael killed himself, and Hyrcanus was mutilated which rendered him unfit to be High Priest. Herod tried to hold out against them but lacked an adequate army, and with the eventual fall of Jerusalem, Antigonus was crowned king. Herod withdrew to the desert fortress of Masada, by the shores of the Dead Sea. He took his family there, including his wife-to-be Mariamne, the daughter of Alexander and granddaughter of Hyrcanus II, whom he wed in 37 BC the same year that Jerusalem fell to his forces, and leaving his family behind escaped to the Nabataeans.

Herod made his way to Rome. The Romans decided Hyrcanus was unfit to rule and Antigonus viewed as a usurper therefore the throne of Judaea was apparently vacant. Octavian and Mark Antony proposed Herod should be named king of the Jews, the Senate concurred. To endear him to his subjects and also to add to the non-Jewish element in his realm, western Idumaea and the domains of the Samaritans were annexed. Although Herod counted his reign from his investiture as king and ally of Rome in 40 BC, three years were to elapse before he could finally establish his claim.

Herod landed at Ptolemais (Acre) and launched his campaign. He managed to take the port of Jaffa, and continued on to Masada to free his family. He then mounted a siege against Jerusalem during which time he also managed to seize Sepphoris (39–38 BC). From Galilee he joined Mark Antony at Samosata on the Euphrates, an act of loyalty that won him great praise and support from Rome. In 37 BC he finally crushed all resistance in Jerusalem and the city fell to him, although the number of people killed in the process was excessive: Antigonus was put to death by Mark Antony and Hasmonaean rule ended.

The task that now faced Herod was no easy one for he had to strengthen his position with the Jews. The Hasmonaean dynasty had been a popular one, as they had represented national independence, with their demise as well as the purging of the aristocracy, the original Sadducees, the Jews had little more than contempt for their new king, the 'Edomite slave' as they called him. Although he thought of himself as a Jew he was not of priestly descent therefore not eligible to hold the office of High Priest, so he chose men for this position whom he could manipulate, and whom he regularly replaced, so creating a new Sadducean aristocracy, one that was totally faithful to the king.

However, the greatest threat came not from within his own lands but from the eastern Mediterranean. Antony and the Egyptian queen Cleopatra VII were hoping to restore the Pharaonic dominion of Asia; Herod lost the coastal area as well as the palm groves of Jericho when Antony decided to give them to Cleopatra. Herod was in a precarious position and could have lost everything. However, in 31 BC the Roman west, led by Octavian (later the emperor Augustus), defeated

Antony and Cleopatra at the battle of Actium, off the Greek mainland.

Herod did not take part in the battle but went to Rhodes and managed to persuade Octavian his loyalty to Antony in the past was a guarantee that, from that moment on, he would be loyal to Octavian. Octavian was soon to be styled Augustus and conferred in the position of 'First Among Equals', in effect master of the Roman world. Herod's bold move had paid off for he received confirmation of his kingship and later, when Augustus made a visit to Judaea, after the final annexation of Egypt, he granted him the entire coast from Gaza to Strato's Tower (Caesarea) except Ascalon, together with the towns of Gadara and Hippos, east of the Jordan. In 23 BC he was assigned large areas beyond the Jordan up to and including the Hauran Mountains, and three years later was given the Golan as far as the source of the Jordan at Paneas.

Augustus' victory brought with it an influx of wealth and prosperity to the empire from which Herod greatly benefitted. The middle years of his reign saw the political and economic consolidation of his rule. His buildings activities were prolific, made possible by the great fortune he had amassed from taxes and business deals such as the exploitation of the Cyprus copper mines.

Herod's kingdom comprised two units, first the 'king's country' ruled directly through governors of the provinces of Galilee, Judaea and Peraea. Each province was divided into toparchies, which were 20 in total; each toparchy consisted of several villages. Also in this unit were the royal estates in the Jezreel Valley, the military districts beyond Jordan and the colonies of veterans at Gaba and Heshbon.

The second unit consisted of the Hellenized cities, some of which were grants from Rome to Herod; the others being cities that Herod had established or revived. The most famous of these were the port of Caesarea, Samaria (Sebaste) inland and another Caesarea at Paneas. All of these cities enjoyed local autonomy, although they were supervised by one of the king's officials.

In Judaea, Herod acted with a double purpose. He naturally wanted to provide for his own security, so he built or rebuilt the fortresses of Masada, Hyrcania and Herodium, a fortified palace in Jerusalem and the Antonia fortress, which commanded the Temple Mount. Herod also needed to show he was a worthy monarch and to this end he undertook the refurbishment of the Temple.

Although Herod's enthusiasm 'for all things Greek' cannot be underestimated, as a client king of Rome, Herod was, to a certain extent, duty bound to prepare his subjects for assimilation into the Roman Empire using Graeco-Roman culture as his main instrument. In 28/27 BC Herod introduced certain Hellenistic activities to Judaea, for example the Actian games, celebrating Augustus' defeat of Antony and Cleopatra at Actium. The games included musical compositions, horse races, athletic contests, wild beast contests, and were to be held every four years in Jerusalem. Three buildings were erected to accommodate these events, a hippodrome in the city on the south side of the Temple, and two others outside the city walls. To some Jews however, this was seen as a step too far towards the Hellenization of their country, especially the gymnastic and wrestling competitions. This sort of activity had been a major political issue at the time of the Maccabean war, over a century earlier. It was regarded as symbolic of the pagan Hellenism that it had been the purpose of the rebellion to eradicate. This was something that pious Jews felt very strongly about.

Herod also wanted his buildings to be magnificent but was faced with the problem of depicting human or animal forms on the sculptured reliefs, a practice that would flout the second commandment. So, instead he unadvisedly adorned some of his buildings with representations of trophies, containing armour and weapons, also anathema to the Jews. Herod's schemes aroused so much animosity that an attempt was made, unsuccessfully, to assassinate him.

Therefore, within his own kingdom Herod had little scope for self-expression so had to look to the Greek cities to the west of Palestine and beyond. In Samaria, the corridor between the Greek cities of the west and Judaea to the east, Herod founded the city of Sebaste, named after his patron, the emperor Augustus. Caesarea, on the coast, was another city that benefited his kingdom greatly, opening up a new port that allowed access to fresh trading routes.

Herod was probably one of the greatest benefactors of the ancient Near East; his list of benefactions to gentile cities is long and imposing. Josephus tells us Herod's benefactions within Palestine included the Temple of Augustus at Paneion, near the River Jordan, the foundation of Agrippium, Antipatris, Cypros and Phasaelis.[2] He provided gymnasia for Tripolis, Byblos and Damascus, and numerous buildings in Berytus, Tyre and Sidon, not counting numerous other benefactions to cities in the Greek east. Yet, it appears he won the gratitude of the Greeks alone. Josephus tells us his own people continued to despise him. The Pharisee Sameas advocated the acceptance of his rule only on the grounds of divine punishment.

Within Judaea Herod had to confine himself to other acts, pious ones. He is credited with the construction of the Patriarchs' tombs in Hebron as well as building a memorial to Abraham two miles from Hebron. However, his greatest achievement was the rebuilding of the Temple, which commenced circa 20 BC, some two years after Herod's initial announcement of the project. Not everyone was ready to accept that this project would come to fruition; Herod was required to prove the feasibility of it before it could commence. To allay fears he further promised not to pull down any of the Temple buildings until the materials for rebuilding were in place.

He employed thousands of workmen on this enterprise and trained priests as masons and carpenters since the Law prohibited laymen from entering the Temple building itself. Although, according to Josephus, Herod repeatedly referred to this work as a pious enterprise his Jewish subjects seem to have been unconvinced of his sincerity and felt his real motivation for the building of the Temple was remorse he felt for killing so many Jewish scholars. As one scholar has pointed out:

> This seems to emphasise the dichotomy of his era. His place in the Roman Empire depended upon his governance of the Jews; he felt bound therefore to respect the religious views of the main body of them. On the other hand, he was convinced that if no compromise were reached between Judaism and Hellenism there would be a catastrophe and the first victim would be his dynasty and all that he had striven to accomplish. Hence the bridging of the gap between the Jews and the world about them was his principal aim.[3]

Herod lived to a ripe old age, nearing 70 when he was struck down by a series of horrific ailments. The end of his reign was as bloody as the beginning having executed several of his sons. He left Antipater to succeed him, however five days before his death he also had him executed. Herod died unmourned by his family and hated by the whole nation. He was buried in Herodium.

With the death of Herod in 4 BC a series of countrywide revolts broke out. The royal army with the assistance of Varus the Roman governor of Syria managed to quell them. The problem of succession was settled in Rome when Augustus divided the realm between Herod's remaining sons. To the eldest Archelaus he granted Judaea, Samaria and the coastal cities, including Caesarea but not Gaza. The second son, Herod Antipas, governed two purely Jewish but separate areas: Galilee and Jewish Transjordan (the Perea). The third son Philip Herodes ruled mainly over the gentile areas east of the river. Archelaus lasted for only nine years and was finally deposed; Roman prefects then ruled his territories. Antipas remained until AD 39 when he was deposed by the emperor Caligula. Philip died peacefully earlier.

In the final years before the war with Rome, Jews had become divided in their attitude to Roman authority. The three main groups comprised the Herodian party and the Sadducees, the Temple aristocracy, and the Zealots. The Herodians were prepared to go further when it came to adopting Hellenistic culture than the Sadducees whose status depended on the Temple and its ritual. However, both were aware that collaboration with Rome offered the best chance of survival, for them as well as their people. The Zealots were the uncompromising faction who fervently believed in Jewish nationalism, and in between the two extremes were the Pharisees a minor group not included in the main parties.

The grandson of Herod, Herod Agrippa I was the spokesman of compromise. He had been brought up in Rome in the imperial household and succeeded in winning the favours of the emperors Caligula and his successor Claudius. In AD

37 Caligula gave him the lands that once belonged to his uncle Philip, and when Antipas was deposed he was also given his lands. Claudius bestowed Judaea and Samaria on him in AD 41; this amounted to nearly all the lands originally held by his grandfather. However, his rule was short-lived as he died three years later. Claudius pronounced his 17-year-old son Agrippa II his successor but as he was still a minor, procuratorial rule was reinstated in Judaea.

Rome did not fully grasp the complexity of the country or of its people. According to the classification referred to by Strabo, the ancient geographer Judaea belonged to the third class of imperial provinces, i.e. those placed under governors of equestrian rank.[4] It was those provinces where a strong individual culture or lack of it, which made the usual implementation of regulations impossible, that were controlled by a junior officer of equestrian rank. Egypt is a prime example of such a province but the same criteria applied to those territories that were inhabited by semi-barbarous peoples.[5]

From the start the choice of procurator appears to have been inept: Pilate was responsible for two major infringements that fuelled the fires of discontent. First, when he brought the legionary standards into the Holy city of Jerusalem, seen as an act of sacrilege, and second when he proceeded to remove money from the Jerusalem Temple to help finance the building of an aqueduct, which led to violence. Nevertheless, there were some outstandingly able procurators, such as the renegade Jew Tiberius Alexander, however the last two procurators Albinus and Florus were rapacious and incompetent and provoked mounting unrest. Finally the majority of the nation chose open warfare against Rome.

The amount of contemporary material available for Roman Palestine far surpasses that for any other province in this period, with the possible exception of Egypt, and is invaluable to historians in terms of understanding how the Roman provinces functioned, or more precisely how the Roman government dealt with diverse or unruly societies.[6] The vast majority of information comes from one source, the Jewish historian Josephus. We have supplementary contemporary material from Philo, an Alexandrian Jew, who records two episodes in the history of the province in his *Legatio* and of course the New Testament from which we also glean additional incidental information.

From the Roman perspective however, there is little material; Suetonius, the biographer, mentions the fortunes of Vespasian and Titus in Judaea. Tacitus in his *Histories* affords mere glimpses into the situation in Judaea, although it must be stressed that the relevant parts of his work are lost. When he does mention events in Judaea he does so in order to show up the misconduct of the procurators; otherwise, according to Tacitus, 'all was quiet under the reign of Tiberius'.[7] However, his views concerning the Jewish race seem to reflect the then popular conception of this alien nation. According to him the practices of the Jews were 'sinister and revolting' and Jewish belief was 'paradoxical and degraded'.[8]

Only when a major war developed, involving two future emperors and four legions did Tacitus deem the province important enough to record some of the details. It is not that he was lacking in his duty as an historian but simply in Roman eyes, Judaea was unimportant, and the riots and rebellions that took place there were of little consequence within the framework of the whole of the empire.

The most frequently asked question of all is why did the Jewish revolt against Rome happen? What caused the Jews to plunge headlong into this calamitous revolt against such a powerful adversary? The answer still remains elusive, despite the fact there is a substantial amount of source material available for the period. The problem lies mainly in the fact that the majority of evidence available comes from one source, *Jewish War*, written by Flavius Josephus. The works of Josephus have been the subject of controversy amongst scholars in recent times. The ambiguity of Josephus' position, first as a Jewish leader of a rebellion, then as, 'a man who assisted his former enemy and was paid for it',[9] has caused many scholars to incline to view his accounts as too personalized for serious consideration. Others believe he still makes a valuable contribution to our understanding of this period of history, despite the fact that his accounts are prone to bias and full of inconsistencies, especially the overlapping accounts in *Life* and *Jewish War* concerning his role in Galilee. In order to examine the Jewish war with Rome it will be necessary to use Josephus' works and while they may tell us about the situation in Judaea consideration must be given to the role that Josephus played in the events he describes and briefly try to evaluate whether his own personal circumstances may have affected his accounts of the revolt.

2

Josephus and his Histories

I will state the facts accurately and impartially. (Jewish War 1:7)

Flavius Josephus is probably the most enigmatic of all ancient historians. A multi-faceted character; he was a Jew, priest, scholar, rebel military commander, traitor, Roman citizen and author (under Imperial Roman patronage). What actual information we have concerning Josephus' life comes entirely from his own writings, partly from his autobiography *Life* (*Vita*), and partly from other morsels of information that are scattered throughout the pages of *Jewish War* (*Bellum Judaicum*).

He tells us he was born Joseph ben Mattiyahu in Jerusalem in AD 37, the child of an aristocratic priestly family, descended on his mother's side from royal blood, the Hasmoneans or Maccabeans. He tells us nothing more about his mother's family but continues in his narration to give an account of his paternal lineage. His early education was a purely religious one based on the Torah, reflecting the training appropriate for a future priest. He would have us believe he was something of a child prodigy who the chief priests and leading city figures would seek out for advice:

> While still a mere boy, about fourteen years old, I won universal applause for my love of letters; insomuch that the chief priests and leading men of the city used constantly to come to me for precise information on some particular in our ordinances.[1]

At the age of 16 he decided to go in search of a suitable religious sect that would accommodate his intellectual needs. At that time in Judaea there were three major religious sects, Pharisees, Sadducees and Essenes, and Josephus tells us he spent three years gaining personal experience of each. It seems highly likely this must have entailed only a cursory foray into the different groups; for example in order to become a member of the Essene sect one had to spend three years solely with them in order to achieve any level of competence, this would have been impossible if, as Josephus says, he also spent three years in the desert as the disciple of Bannus the aesthetic:

With him I lived for three years and, having accomplished my purpose, returned to the city. Being now in my nineteenth year I began to govern my life by the rules of the Pharisees.

This kind of inconsistency is a characteristic of all Josephus' writings, and something one must be aware of when assessing what he has to say about the later tumultuous events that happened in his country. According to his account in *Life*, at the age of 19 he finally chose to govern his life by the rules of the Pharisees, a sect having points of resemblance to that which the Greeks call the Stoic school. The identification with Stoicism reveals an ignorance of and indifference to philosophy and is an easy, though inaccurate, way of trying to communicate with a Greek audience.[2] This is somewhat surprising as throughout his works, especially in *Jewish War* and *Antiquities*, he displays a profound dislike towards them. However, it is possible when he was writing his *Life* he decided to emphasize his earlier connections with the Pharisees for by then they had become extremely popular, and no doubt Josephus craved popular support.

He tells us nothing more about himself until he reached the age of 26, when he had his first contact with Rome (circa AD 63). He was sent there on a mission to the emperor Nero (who sent him there he does not say) to secure the release of several priests, despatched as prisoners on trifling charges by Felix, the procurator of Judaea at the time. While in Rome, Josephus was afforded an introduction to Poppaea Sabina, consort of the emperor Nero, and he wasted no time in trying to solicit her aid in his mission. He must have made a favourable impression on her for he tells us she gave him large gifts, but fails to say what they were, indeed they may well have been gifts destined for the Temple, as Poppaea was known to be a Jewish sympathizer.

On his return to Judaea he found his country on the verge of rebellion against Rome. He attempted to pacify members of the war party but found himself powerless trying to restrain them. They apparently would not heed his warnings of the dire consequences that would ensue should they persist in confronting the might of Rome, so fearing he would be regarded as a traitor he sought asylum in the Temple along with several other like-minded individuals. Jointly they appeared to sympathize with the rebel cause while at the same he time tried to persuade them to act defensively and let Rome make the first move. By acting in this way, Josephus tells us:

We had hopes that ere long Cestius (the governor of Syria) would come up with a large army and quell the revolution.[3]

Although Josephus leaves a full account of the events that finally led to open rebellion, he actually played no part in them. After Cestius' disastrous foray to

Jerusalem, the rebel government appointed Josephus to take command of the two Galilees and the city of Gamala. Josephus was barely 30 years of age and had little military experience, but according to his account in *Life* he was sent, along with two other priests, Joazar and Judas:

> To induce the disaffected to lay down their arms and to impress on them the desirability of reserving these for the picked men of the nation. The latter, so it was decided were to have their weapons constantly in readiness for future contingencies, but should wait and see what action the Romans would take.[4]

In *Life* he tells us his mission was a failure, because he was unable to persuade the rebels to give up their arms. Yet, the same account in *JW* presents us with significant disparities; in this account it seems, he was given from the start an important military command in Galilee, and he speaks about the training he gave his men based on Roman military lines (although how he had acquired such knowledge he does not say).

We also read in *Life* how he comes into conflict with an important Galilean, John of Gischala. John accused him of being a traitor and sent to his friends in Jerusalem to entreat the assembly to have Josephus removed from his post and appoint him in his place. The High Priest Ananus and Simon, son of Gamaliel sent a secret deputation of four, including apparently one of Josephus' former companions, Joazar, to supersede him. Josephus outwitted this deputation, made counter-representations to Jerusalem and got himself reinstated.

It is not clear why he was appointed to this post in the first place to oversee a distracted province, given his pacifist and pro-Roman tendencies; the capital, Sepphoris was staunchly pro-Roman but refused to have any dealings with him; Gamala remained loyal while Tiberias was a constant hotbed of trouble and faction fighting. Josephus' motives are also questionable, and from the evidence he supplies suggests he was playing a double waiting game. He tells how he trained volunteers and fortified cites and villages under his protection, yet he also tells us when he received a request from John of Gischala to authorize him to seize the imperial corn stored in the villages of Upper Galilee he replied: 'I intended to reserve the corn either for the Romans or for my own use'. Therefore it is little wonder Josephus was suspected of harbouring traitorous thoughts to betray the country to the enemy. According to this account it was the rebels, or as he refers to them the 'brigands', who forced his hand and compelled him to put himself at the head of the war party in Galilee, or be superseded.

The rest of story is taken up in *JW*, when in the spring of AD 67, with the advance of the Roman army under the command of the general Vespasian, Josephus, who had been deserted by most of his volunteer army, was forced to take refuge in the fortified town of Jotapata and withstand a siege.

The incident at Jotapata, which he recounts in Chapter 3 of *JW*, is probably the most singularly embarrassing chapter in all of Josephus' works. He tells how, when the town was besieged by the Romans he and 40 other notables under his command hid in a cave. Vespasian offered him a pardon (i.e. he could surrender and not be killed) because he was a general, but his companions preferred to commit suicide rather than fall into Roman hands. After haranguing his companions with a long rhetorical speech on the sinfulness of suicide (which failed to move them), he agreed to their suicide pact. He proposed the drawing of lots to decide the order of mutual killing. So, they drew lots; one-by-one they carried out the killing of their comrades until only Josephus and one other person were left. Josephus recounts with great pride his ingenious duping of his countrymen and makes it clear he 'had counted the numbers by cunning and thereby misled them all'. If Josephus had arranged the selection using a circular count then it has been proven that a clever manipulator could contrive the order in which to place himself within the circle in order to survive. In more modern times mathematicians called this method of counting a 'Josephus count' (*Josephus-spiel*), and it became one of the most popular arithmetical problems of the Middle Ages.[5]

Having contrived to ensure his survival, Josephus was brought before Vespasian to whom he related a prophetic dream he had in which Vespasian was to become emperor of Rome, and a new Flavian dynasty established; the prophecy according to the Roman historian Suetonius was attested to by a pagan witness.[6] Incidentally, in the *Talmud* this prophecy was attributed to the prophet Johannan b. Zakkai who was an inside witness to the siege of Jerusalem. We are led to believe because of this he received clemency from the future emperor; even so he was still a prisoner. Shortly after his prediction came true: the eventful and bloody year AD 68–69, when hostilities in Judaea were suspended, witnessed the death of the emperor Nero, followed in quick succession by three emperors before finally Vespasian took matters into his own hands and was proclaimed emperor by his eastern legions.

One of Vespasian's first acts as emperor was to release the man who had prophesied his future success. Josephus accompanied him to Alexandria; from there he returned in AD 70 to Judaea with Vespasian's son, Titus, to witness the siege of Jerusalem and to act as mediator, circuiting the walls of the city trying to persuade the Jews to surrender; it was only Titus' protection that saved him from the wrath of his countrymen who once again saw him as a betrayer of their country. In gratitude Titus presented him with a tract of land outside Jerusalem and some sacred books; Josephus also managed to obtain from the conqueror of his people the liberation of some his friends including his father and brother. He then accompanied Titus to Rome, never to return to Judaea.

Josephus tells us a little about his domestic life at this time:

> At this period I divorced my wife, being displeased at her behaviour. She had borne me three children, of whom two died; one, whom I named Hyrcanus, is still alive. Afterwards I married a woman of Jewish extraction who had settled in Crete. She came of very distinguished parents, indeed the most notable in that country. In character she surpassed many of her sex, as her subsequent life showed. By her I had two sons, Justus the elder, and then Simonides, surnamed Agrippa. Such is my domestic history.[7]

However, to his own people he always remained a traitor, *the traitor of Jerusalem,* as some have called him;[8] and for many the mere fact he could write about the incident at Jotapata in the way he did, meant he lost all credibility as an historian.

Josephus spent the remaining 30 years or more in Rome as a client of the Flavians and was commissioned to write the history of their triumph over the Jews. He presented his work *Jewish War* to the emperor for official approval, which he got; Titus affixed his seal and ordered it to be made available to the public. He was awarded full Roman citizenship, took a Roman name, Flavius (after his patrons) Josephus, was given a lodging in the former palace of Vespasian and a pension, newly instituted by the emperor. He spent the rest of his life in Rome devoting his time to writing until his death circa AD 100.

However, even in the safety of his new homeland, he was constantly coming under attack from his countrymen, even amongst his own household. He was accused of subsidizing a Jewish revolt in Cyrene, slandered by his son's tutor, and finally verbally attacked by his rival, Justus of Tiberias. This was perhaps the most damaging incident of his career. Justus was a rival historian, who in his history threw out the accusation that Josephus, during his command in Galilee, had been responsible for the revolt in his [Justus'] native Tiberias. Justus' history has not survived so there is no way of knowing what was said or how much truth there was in the accusations. However, these exposures seriously threatened the security of his position and well as sales of his works.

On the death of his patron, the emperor Titus in AD 79 he finally shook off his Roman fetters and became the historian and apologist of his people. However, he was still part of the imperial circle, he tells us:

> The treatment I received from the emperors continued unaltered. Domitian succeeded Titus and added to my honours. He punished my Jewish accusers, and for a similar offence gave orders for the chastisement of a slave, a eunuch and my son's tutor. He also exempted my property in Judaea from taxation – a mark of the highest honour to the privileged individual. Moreover, Domitia, Caesar's wife, never ceased conferring favours on me.[9]

Nevertheless, he never won his countrymen's affection, it was Rome that perpetuated his memory; ancient sources tell us there was a statue erected to him in Rome (now lost) in his honour.[10] His works profoundly influenced the early Church Fathers, especially Jerome who praised him as a second Livy (*Epistula ad Eustochium* 22.35). The *Testimonium Flavianum* is a Slavonic version of *War*, apparently made in the eleventh century AD and in which there are a number of additions to the original Greek version. These additional passages contain references to John the Baptist and Jesus. Recent scholarship indicates the work was utilized by Christians in the ideological struggle against the Khazars who had converted to Judaism in the eighth century AD. Because of this work Josephus was regarded as having borne witness to the miracles and ministry of Jesus, his Messiahship and resurrection, so it not surprising his works appeared alongside those of the Church Fathers. During the Middle Ages he was regarded as a polymath, an authority in such diverse fields as biblical exegesis, arithmetic, astronomy, geography, etymology and Jewish theology. Certainly his works, especially *Jewish War* have remained popular up to modern times, and have inspired writers such as Voltaire, Petrarch, and in the twentieth century a trilogy of novels by Leon Feuchtwanger.

However, one question still remains; was Josephus really a traitor or a man of vision who believed the way forward for his people was collaboration rather than confrontation with Rome? The question has never been fully resolved and even now is still a subject of controversy. In October 1992 Israeli television devoted a whole evening to the debate; Josephus was put on trial for treason. Once again it appears Josephus' skill for survival served him well with later generations also; the outcome was the acquittal of the accused for lack of evidence.

Josephus wrote four works in Greek: two were written towards the end of his life, *Against Apion* (*Contra Aponium*, published c. AD 96) and the rather misleadingly entitled *Life* (*Vita* published c. AD 93/4), which is not a true autobiography but an apologia. The historical writings are earlier and consist of two overlapping works, The *Jewish War* (*Bellum Judaicum*) and *Jewish Antiquities* (*Antiquitates Judaicae*), of which *War* is the earlier and by far the more interesting (published c. AD 79 and AD 93/4 respectively). Originally there was an Aramaic version of the *JW*, which has not survived; all we know of it is what Josephus tells us. He says he wrote an Aramaic version not for a gentile audience, but to warn near eastern neighbours of the folly of hasty action against the might of Rome. The Aramaic version was widely distributed among the *barbarians of the interior* of Asia, and could well have been a commissioned work. Josephus was uniquely qualified to do the job. His position as a member of the priestly aristocracy ensured his credibility with his own people, he also had access to documentation, but above all he could address the intended readership in their own language, Aramaic. Until such time a copy emerges we cannot ascertain whether or not there were substantial differences between the content of the two works. Fortunately for posterity, he decided to rewrite the work in Greek.

The books that have survived are, in style and content, Hellenistic Greek works, written for the Greek-speaking population, and owe their survival to the fact they were composed in or translated into Greek. Josephus wrote, not in the common literary language of the Hellenistic age, New Testament Greek, but in the revived Greek of classical Athens. A notable achievement considering he was a Palestinian Jew, not an Alexandrian one whose first language would have been Greek, a Palestinian Jew's knowledge of Greek would have been somewhat superficial in comparison. Linguistically his achievement did not go unrecognized, seven centuries later the Byzantine Patriarch, Photius commented on the purity of his language.

Josephus was similarly proud of his achievement: he says, at the close of *Antiquities*: 'I make bold to say that no one else whether Jew or alien, could, with the best will in the world have produced a work of such accuracy as this for Greek readers'.[11] Nevertheless he had collaborators to assist him with the translation, and to whom he makes one passing reference in *Against Apion*. The extent of their contribution is a matter for debate amongst scholars, however there is nothing other than assumption to suggest the collaborators played any substantial part in the composition despite some contrary assertions.[12] Josephus wrote in the Greek tradition of historiography, modelling his style upon the political history of the Greek historian Thucydides, with emphasis on the superiority of eyewitness accounts. The Greek historians Herodotus and Thucydides, and the Roman historian Sallust, all wrote about events that either they witnessed themselves or had reported to them by contemporary witnesses. The kind of detachment Thucydides achieved was rare and inevitably personal bias often found its way into this style of historical writing. The model for the composition of the *Antiquities* was the work of the Greek historian Dionysius of Halicarnassus, who published his *Antiquities of the Romans* in 7 BC, contained in 20 books, precisely the same number that Josephus employed for his work. However unlike Dionysius, Josephus was faced with the need to be an apologist as well as an historian, and the difficulties this presented must have been considerable. It is one thing to write about the Roman rise to power, quite another to write about the history of a nation that was disliked, vilified and considered alien by the most powerful empire in the ancient world.

We cannot be certain what books Josephus read or what sources he used. If the Epaphroditus to whom Josephus dedicated all his later works was his patron, after the death of Titus, then it could be the same man as the learned Greek grammarian. There were two contemporary men with the same uncommon name. This one is commemorated in an inscription: the other was a freedman and secretary to the emperor Nero. We know this man was reputed to have amassed a private library consisting of 30,000 books, which would have put Josephus in a far better position to acquire information than many of his contemporaries. In his defence it must be stressed there is little reason to suppose books existed that actually covered certain periods of his histories, e.g. the early decades of the first century after the death of Herod the Great.

However, we can be fairly confident about some of his sources. For the greater part of the *Antiquities*, the period down to the Maccabees, his main source of information was the Bible. Apart from the Pentateuch, Judges, Joshua and possibly Ruth, he relied heavily upon the Greek rather than Hebrew or Aramaic texts. This calls into question the level of Josephus' own biblical scholarship, Josephus seems ignorant about the smaller mistakes that occur, no doubt due to errors in translation; if he were well versed in the Hebrew text this should not have occurred so frequently. One scholar has queried his use of the Hebrew Bible because of this reliance on the Greek text and not without some justification.

We can also trace the influences of the *haggadah*, (older legends) particularly in his account of Moses and the Patriarchs. However, it appears he employed not only oral tradition but also supplemented stories derived from earlier Hellenistic versions of Biblical history from such writers as Demetrius and Artapanus. For the Law he followed the Palestinian *halakah*[13] and we cannot overlook the possibility he would have made use of the meticulously kept priestly documents. Other non-Biblical sources are also cited to supplement or corroborate individual events.[14]

For the two centuries preceding the Hasmoneans there was little Biblical authority. Herod the Great had his own personal biographer, Nicolaus of Damascus upon whom Josephus relied heavily. If we compare his account of Herod in *JW* with that in *Antiquities,* we can note differences that have serious implications concerning his abilities as a critical historian. For example in *Antiquities* his portrayal of Herod is one of exhaustive flattery, almost a straight copy of Nicolaus of Damascus' work. However, in *JW*, he employed a hostile antagonism towards the king that reflected the attitude of the people of Jerusalem.[15]

When writing about the Roman period he would have had access to official Roman documents, and no doubt while he lived in Rome would have become familiar with the official *commentarii* (commander's log books) of the emperors Vespasian and Titus. There is much credence given to the importance of these documents by some scholars, especially when Josephus is describing the destruction of Jerusalem in AD 70.[16] However, this is at variance with Josephus' own account in *Against Apion*[17] where he states he used the notes he made at the time along with statements from deserters about the situation inside the city. Consideration must also be given to the fact he may have consulted the works of Strabo, Polybius and Philo, although in the case of the latter there is evidence to suggest this may not have been the case.

The use Josephus made of his sources has often given cause for concern amongst scholars, especially with regard to his accuracy and reliability. It is evident he used source material for his own purposes and was not above changing or substituting material in order to emphasize his own personal ideology. His use of Biblical sources overall is fairly accurate. Nevertheless, he frequently used the Bible as an apologetic and often made modifications. He omitted items that may have caused offence and his aim appears to have been to present Jewish history in the best possible light. A good example can be seen in his account in *Antiquities* of Daniel's interpretation of Nebuchadnezzar's dream. Josephus gives this version:

> but their empire will be destroyed by another king from the west, clad in bronze, and this power will be ended by still another, like iron, that will have dominion forever through its iron nature, which he said is harder than that of gold, silver or bronze. And Daniel also revealed to the king the meaning of the stone, but I have not thought it proper to relate this, since I am expected to write of what is past and done and not what is to be.[18]

What Josephus omitted was the detail that the fourth kingdom was 'of iron mixed with miry clay'; and what was not proper to relate at all was that 'in the days of those kings shall God of heaven set up a kingdom which shall never be destroyed ... but it shall break in pieces and consume all these kingdoms, and it shall stand forever'.[19]

The Jewish interpretation current at the time was that the fourth kingdom was Rome, which would be overthrown at the coming of the Messiah. Writing in Rome as a Roman citizen, under Roman patronage, Josephus found himself in a difficult situation and would have seen little option other than to omit or change the text. Obviously from Josephus' point of view there was a good apologetic reason for tampering with the original. Another characteristic of Josephus is that he used good stories for apologetic ends, regardless of whether or not they were true, for example, Alexander's visit to Jerusalem in *JA*.

For the decades preceding the revolt and subsequent war with Rome, Josephus had little source material and relied upon his own recollection of events. By comparing the texts of the two works *JA* and *JW*, where they overlap historically, it becomes apparent, at such times as these Josephus was at a loss with his work. Overall they become patchy and incomplete and he only appears to regain confidence in his writing when he reaches the period in which he was personally involved.

There is almost universal assent he composed *JW* for his Flavian patrons and even the title of the work reflects his pro-Roman biases. Some scholars believe it can be misleading to accept this concept at face value.[20] Like many ancient historians the speeches Josephus writes can be vehicles for his own thoughts. One speech in particular is worthy of mention in this context. The speech is contained in Book 7 of *JW*, here he puts into the mouth of Eleazar ben Yair, the leader of the Zealots in their last desperate stand against the might of Rome on Herod's rock fortress of Masada, a speech that seems specifically to have been created as a counterweight to the Roman triumph over his people It is more powerful in its exposition, not only that but Josephus has also chosen this incident to provide the climax to his work. It appears 'the pull of the Flavians is not made to supersede earlier loyalties' and something worth serious consideration.[21] This speech, however, has other connotations. Josephus also uses this method as a way of laying the blame for the whole affair on the Zealots, and here in the final chapter he makes them confess their sin. This is not to say he exonerates the Romans or shows bias on their behalf, quite the reverse; he is attempting to show his gentile audience that only one section of the Jewish people could be held responsible for the calamitous events, the notorious Zealots, whose way led only to death. Even though in Josephus' eyes they were wrong he still ennobles them by making them prefer death rather than servitude. The emphasis seems to be that the Jewish people themselves brought about their destruction;[22] Rome was merely the instrument by which God punished them for their crimes.

Whether or not the work was commissioned, Josephus appears to have had his own motivation for writing *JW*. There had been other accounts of the war published after the event and Josephus found them all inadequate. There were accounts written by people who had not participated in events, and others written by military veterans who recounted the great heroics of the victors while at the same time playing down the role of the Jews, something, according to Josephus, was a deplorable state of affairs: 'I fail to see how the conquerors of so puny a people deserve to be accounted great'. For Josephus there was only one recourse and that was to write an account himself, who better than someone who had participated on both sides? As he says the only historians deserving of praise are those who undertake

> the work of committing to writing events which have not been previously recorded and of commending to posterity the history of one's own time who use fresh materials and make the framework of history their own.[23]

As none of the other accounts have survived, Josephus' *JW* is the only complete work concerning the period leading up to the revolt against Rome and with little else by which to judge the veracity of the work, we can only compare this version with similar accounts in his other works to ascertain its reliability. Instead of finding his recollections are basically sound and accurate, often we are presented with frustrating discrepancies, especially between his accounts in *Life* and *JW* concerning the early stages of the rebellion. In these accounts he deals with events in Galilee in which he played a significant role. Yet his recollections of this period appear oddly vague, and we are left with the impression we are not being presented with the whole truth. These discrepancies cannot easily be accounted for and have prompted scholars to offer a variety of explanations, none of which as yet, has proved satisfactory. It would appear Josephus is only reliable when he does not use his own personal religious or political biases to emphasize a particular reason for a course of action.[24]

In order to assess the reasons he gives for the revolt it is necessary to bear in mind that Josephus is capable of using information for his own purposes and omitting anything he considered irrelevant or embarrassing. The proximity of Josephus to events he describes would obviously account for some inevitable personal bias. However, the causes he cites for the war can be divided into two separate categories, the accelerating causes and the immediate causes, and need to be examined in order to discover why, according to Josephus, the conflict with Rome came about.

3

The Causes of Revolution According to Josephus (I)

The ostensible pretext for war was out of proportion to the
magnitude of the disasters to which it led. (JW 2:284)

With the exception of the Peloponnesian War in fourth-century BC Greece, chronicled by the historian Thucydides, there is no other war in antiquity for which such an elaborate account survives and for this we are indebted to Josephus. However, there are a lot of serious omissions in his narratives and the different social and political structures, as well as the differences in culture, make it extremely difficult to draw comparisons with other revolts within the Roman Empire. We may be inclined to agree with historians when they say there was not one single cause for the revolt but an amalgamation of reasons that combined to bring about the final confrontation with Rome.[1] The reasons, accepted by most scholars are; socio/economic problems (however, should we believe that only the Jews were poor? No gentiles appear to have taken part in this revolt surely they would have done had economic reasons been the sole cause?); fighting between Jews and Gentiles; religious conflicts with Rome; the activities of various extremist groups; the anti-Jewish behaviour of the last Roman procurators; and alienation from the ruling class.[2] Josephus mentions all of these causes at some point and all are perfectly valid when assessing the reasons for conflict with Rome, but they are not entirely satisfactory when trying to evaluate the actual cause of conflict.

According to Josephus' works there appear to have been two stages to the eventual conflict, the accelerating causes and the immediate causes. What becomes apparent in the evidence we have from Josephus is that during the 50s and 60s there was a gradual breakdown in the leadership of the country, both Roman and Jewish. The deplorable handling by the procurator Cumanus (AD 48–52) of the conflict between the Galileans and the Samaritans saw the spread of a breakdown of authority to the countryside, and it was in the countryside that bands of brigands arose who terrorized the populace throughout this period.

The accelerating causes Josephus cites are many and varied. In *JW* he cites conflict within the Jewish community itself,[3] trouble with the Syrian Greek/ Jewish communities,[4] various theological reasons, and in *Life* even goes as far as to lay the blame for the revolt at the door of Justus of Tiberias and his brother (his accuser regarding his behaviour in Galilee). However, two main reasons become prominent throughout his works: first the misadministration of the province by the Roman procurators, and second the behaviour of the dissident Jewish factions, especially the group referred to as the Fourth Philosophy.

The Roman procurators left much to be desired as men of ability, even the Roman historian, Tacitus was not completely unjustified in his biases towards these men. What is surprising is that the tolerance that was shown towards the Diaspora Jews is markedly absent in Judaea.[5] Tacitus' epigram *duravit tamen patientia Iudaeis* (all was quiet in Judaea) is a very telling one. Another failing on the part of the Roman administration was that when capable men were appointed to the post they were inadequately supplied with the necessary military strength to ensure order was kept and this was indeed a serious oversight on the part of Rome, who must surely have been aware this was no 'ordinary' province.

However, the blame was not all one-sided and Josephus does give other instances where Jewish provocation of Roman authority led directly to conflict. Nationalism was a vital issue amongst the Jews and it was the Jews' political as well as their religious fanaticism that made them a difficult people to govern. It would not be unreasonable to reverse Tacitus' remark and say *duravit patientia et Romanis* (all was quiet at Rome).[6] The difficulties involved in governing the Jews were even more apparent when they were massed together in their homeland. Since the rebellion of Judas of Galilee in AD 6, the seeds of dissent had been sown, and although Josephus is writing rather naively when he attributes the cause of the revolt directly to this earlier rebellion, he does hit upon a germ of truth. The doctrines and notions bred out of this rebellion engendered the idea that terrorism and open revolt would inevitably be the only solution against Roman domination. The foundation stones had been laid for the development of divergent terrorist movements throughout the years that followed, which went in no small way to bringing about the final confrontation between the Jews and their Gentile overlords.

One historian has pointed out that Josephus indirectly mentions a variety of possible causes throughout all his works, not just in a few paragraphs of *JW*, but adds that modern scholarship has neglected to do a systematic analysis of them, concentrating instead on the few more major issues.[7] This is a valid statement, yet while this type of analysis would not necessarily clarify the underlying cause of the revolt, it would perhaps go some way to highlighting Josephus' pre-occupation with trying to assess the problems that faced the province.

Many of the causes Josephus cites, either directly or indirectly, revolve around the behaviour of the procurators. He was not against procuratorial rule *per se* and had very clear opinions about how a good procurator should govern; according to him he should be able to control the dissidents, show reverence to all Jewish religious customs and maintain a distance from the cult and Temple. Perhaps more importantly in his eyes, a good procurator devolved responsibility onto the High Priests and persons of note thereby avoiding conflict. This was the ideal, the truth was very different, and Josephus found very few examples of such men who could satisfy the criteria throughout the 60 years of Roman procuratorial rule up to the outbreak of the revolt.

Josephus supplies no information on the procurators for the period AD 6–26 he merely lists, in *JA*, the names of the men who held office during that time. This is unfortunate for as already noted, in AD 6, the seeds of revolt were already being sown by a man named Judas of Galilee, who it appears organized the first anti-Roman party in Judaea. He and a radical Pharisee, Zadok led a revolt, which was quelled by Quintilius Varus who executed 2,000 participants. Further information about this incident may have revealed similarities with later disturbances.[8]

The first procurator to be mentioned by Josephus is Pontius Pilate, to whom Josephus attributes three acts of sacrilege against the Jewish faith. Pilate was the fifth governor of the province of Judaea and held office from AD 26–37. His main responsibilities as governor were primarily military; his official title was *Praefectus Iudaeae* (prefect of Judaea). A mutilated limestone inscription was found in Caesarea in 1961, it commemorated a building erected by Pilate for the emperor Tiberius (known as the Tiberium, but what the building's function was is not certain) and bears out Pilate's title of prefect.

The first incident that caused a public outcry concerned the legionary standards, which Pilate had brought into Jerusalem. Previous procurators had, out of respect for Jewish religious feeling, always chosen for their garrison in the Antonia fortress, close to Temple Mount, standards that contained no medallion bust portraits of the emperor. Pilate decided to exchange these standards with ones that did contain the emperor's portrait, and took them to Jerusalem on the Day of Atonement and Feast of Tabernacles. When the presence of these items (in close proximity to the High Priest's vestments in the Antonia) became known demonstrations ensued. On the pretext of listening to the protestors Pilate summoned the leading men to a tribunal, and then ringed them with soldiers, threatening to kill them if they did not desist. They surprised Pilate by offering themselves willing to the sword, rather than infringe their Law. Pilate rescinded his decision and sent the troops back to Caesarea, but the Jews, although they won a decisive victory now became suspicious so whatever Pilate did from then on would be suspect. Josephus however, gives him credit for promptly withdrawing the troops owing to public pressure.

He followed this act by committing another equally disrespectful one when he allegedly took money from the Temple treasury to help finance the building of an aqueduct; this action resulted in violence, and many Jewish protestors were beaten to death or crushed in the ensuing stampede.[9] A lesser incident occurred when one of his soldiers performed an indecent act within the city; this also resulted in violence.

There is a further incident concerning Pilate that goes unrecorded by Josephus but is mentioned by the Alexandrian Jew and philosopher, Philo in his work *Legatio*.[10] It appears Pilate had gilded shields, dedicated to the emperor Tiberius, attached to the walls of Herod's palace, his residence in Jerusalem. It is a rather bewildering account, inasmuch as even Philo, who was a Jew, is at odds to explain why these shields should have infringed the Law, as they were anionic, unlike the standards that Pilate previously brought into the city. There was no violence this time but the Jews demanded that Pilate produce the emperor Tiberius' authorization for the dedications, so they could appeal to Rome to have them removed. Tiberius reprimanded Pilate and ordered the shields to be removed to the imperial cult temple in Caesarea. The fact Josephus does not mention this incident cannot be dismissed as an oversight, but then, in Josephus' defence, Philo does not mention the episode of the standards, neither does he make any reference to Pilate's flouting of the Jewish religious susceptibilities that Josephus goes to great lengths to emphasize. In Philo's accounts of events in Rome there is evidence that may shed light on this oversight in Josephus' narrative.

In his work *Legatio* Philo speaks of the anti-Semitism of Aelius Sejanus, the Praetorian commander and right-hand man of the emperor Tiberius, and his policy to annihilate the whole Jewish race.[11] The early Christian writer Eusebius uses Philo as a source to support the view that Sejanus' policy was linked with the attack on the Temple and was divine retribution for the crucifixion of Christ. It is possible there was a longer account by Philo that has not survived. Nevertheless it is conceivable Pilate either received instructions from Sejanus to stir up the Jews in order to provoke trouble for the emperor Tiberius, or, more likely, Pilate saw an opportunity to call attention to himself in the hope he would gain favour with Sejanus (who at that time appeared to be on course for higher office, some believe perhaps even emperor). Pilate's actions can certainly seem deliberate rather than misguided. There is further evidence to lend credence to this theory. Pilate issued a series of coins based on Republican coin types which depicted the *simpulum* and *litmus*, pagan objects the Jews found offensive, even more so considering they had to use these coins on a daily basis.[12] The coins can be dated to AD 29/32 and would have been in line with Sejanus' policy.[13] When Sejanus fell from power, Pilate fearing reprisals from the emperor, may have decided to display his loyalty to Tiberius with the dedication of the shields and later the Tiberieum, a unique building in the city of Caesarea. The building may have been a temple, or it may have been a purely secular building such as a portico.

Although this theory affords some explanation for Pilate's behaviour, it does not account for Josephus' omission of the incident. There is no reason to suppose Josephus would have had access to information concerning events in Rome.

What is apparent in Josephus' accounts of Pilate is that it is always the *mob* that confronts him; we never learn what the Jewish *notables* think or do in any of these situations. Yet the episode with the shields demonstrated that Jewish authorities did take action and *could* appeal directly to the emperor *and* receive favourable treatment. Therefore, would Josephus want to show an improvement in the situation when the real intention was to show the gradual breakdown of Roman/ Jewish relations? Or could it be because he could find no rational reason within the Law for the Jewish authorities' outcry over the shields, he chose instead to omit the episode, simply because it did not fit into the pattern he had woven for Pilate, i.e. his flouting of Jewish religious susceptibilities?

There is one other incident Josephus does not mention in his account of Pilate, that of the crucifixion of Christ.[14] It is the Roman historian Tacitus who supplies this information in connection with Christian implication in the fire of Rome during Nero's reign (AD 65). This is the only information Tacitus gives concerning Pilate. According to him *all was quiet* during the reign of Tiberius,[15] hardly a view shared by the Jews. But such statements do reflect the insignificance of Judaea in Roman eyes.

We find further discrepancies when we compare Philo's and Josephus' account of the legate Petronius' actions, when faced with having to implement the next emperor Caligula's wish to have his statue erected in the Temple towards the end of AD 39. In Philo's version Petronius was more indecisive whether or not to implement the order, while in Josephus' version Petronius was inclined from the outset to favour the Jewish supplicants. There are also great discrepancies concerning the dating of the events, with Josephus giving two different accounts in *JW* and *JA*. Josephus' version is also very ornate which tends to make his account a little suspect. On the other hand, Philo's version would seem the more reliable for he was contemporary with events and had some connection to them. He was the leader of one of the embassies sent to the emperor Gaius (Caligula) by the Alexandrian Jews and was in contact, while in Rome, with the Jewish king, Agrippa I who intervened to save the Temple.

Philo also tells us Petronius had studied Judaism before governing those provinces containing Diaspora Jews, so to be better equipped to understand any problems of a religious nature he might encounter. If we read Josephus' account in *JW*, Petronius had to have the Law explained to him in order to understand why the Jews were objecting to the statue being erected in the Temple. Millar points out that Josephus could not have read Philo's account otherwise he would have known about Petronius' knowledge of Judaism.[16] Nevertheless Josephus was probably inclined to portray Petronius as a sympathetic non-Jew, willing to listen to petitioners, rather than someone who was aware of the consequences the action by the emperor could bring. Yet again it suited Josephus' stylistic purpose, and helped to highlight good and bad administrators, in this case Petronius satisfies the criteria for a good administrator. This device is also employed to re-enforce Josephus' belief that compromise between Rome and Judaea could always have been a possibility.

Josephus appears to have been satisfied with the next two procurators, Cuspius Fadus (AD 44?–46) and Tiberius Julius Alexander saying 'they did not interfere with any of the customs of the country and so kept the nation at peace'.[17] In *JA* however, he gives a slightly less positive view, especially referring to an incident concerning Cuspius Fadus, who he says tried to regain control of the High Priests' vestments; he is exonerated by Josephus because he responded to their objections. What really stands out for Josephus is that Cuspius Fadus and Tiberius Julius Alexander both helped rid the country of bandits. He especially notes the efforts of Tiberius Julius Alexander, who executed the sons of Judas of Galilee (the man responsible for the uprisings that followed Quirinius' census in AD 6), after several acts of terrorism. The calm picture Josephus paints hides the fact this was an extremely difficult time for the province. Evidence from Acts tells of a great famine, confirmed by Tacitus taking place in the year AD 51. Josephus makes no mention of it in *JW*; although he does refer to a famine in *JA*, which may be this one. He does not mention the crucifixion of other Jewish rebels, no doubt spurred into rebellion by the famine. It is enough for Josephus the procurator retained control and disciplined the right kind of Jew, without antagonising the wrong ones. Tiberius Julius Alexander was the nephew of Philo and he had renounced his Jewish heritage, he was one of only two procurators of Judaea to go on to achieve higher office, that of Prefect of Egypt. As far as we know the only other procurator to be promoted to a more senior procuratorship and whose later career was also recorded was Albinus (AD 62–64). The fact that Alexander was a Jew helped him maintain control simply by his policy of non-interference with Jewish custom and for this he gets the seal of approval from Josephus.

It is abundantly clear the troubles and difficulties of direct administration from Rome manifested themselves between the years AD 4–6, for 'there was a distinct lack of mutual understanding. The social tensions coupled with the demands of Roman imperial policy and provincial administration were not easily reconcilable with the distinctive character of the Jewish situation'.[18]

The years AD 48–66 saw five procurators holding office. Three of them come in for severe criticism from Josephus. The arrival of Ventidius Cumanus (AD 48–52) marks a turning point in the province's history, for now, according to Josephus, Roman procuratorial rule goes from bad to worse. Cumanus was similar to Pilate in that he also flouted Jewish religious susceptibilities, yet Josephus does not castigate him as much as he does Pilate, rather strange considering Cumanus was even less able to control the situation. Cumanus receives mention in both *JW* and *JA*. The first incident concerns an obscene gesture made by a Syrian soldier on the roof of the Antonia at the time of Passover. Some people even accused

Cumanus of instigating the incident while others called on him to punish the culprit. Finally when some of the angry crowd began pelting the soldiers on the porticoes with stones, Cumanus sent reinforcements down into the enclosure of the Temple precincts; many Jews panicked and there was considerable loss of life in the ensuing stampede. Josephus' reporting of the casualties appears to be excessive; in *JW* the number killed is 30,000. This figure is later amended in *JA* to 20,000.

The next incident involved an attack on an imperial slave on the Joppa/ Jerusalem Road. Cumanus sent troops to the scene of the crime and they were ordered to plunder local villages, probably because he suspected them of being nationalist centres, but more significantly the troops tore up a scroll of the Law and burnt it in full view of the local population. This act of sacrilege almost had the population on the verge of revolt. Only when Cumanus had the offending soldier beheaded was calm restored. The final incident in AD 51 involved armed conflict between Samaritan and Galilean Jews. The inhabitants of a Samaritan village waylaid a group of Galilean pilgrims on their way to Jerusalem and killed a number of them. The Galilean authorities called on Cumanus to have the affair investigated but Cumanus brushed their appeal to one side, saying he had more pressing matters to deal with.

When news of the murders reached Jerusalem anger broke out, the Sanhedrin and other notables tried to intervene and called for moderation from the Galileans and justice from Rome, which they eventually got, but not after more violence had erupted. The Galileans had taken matters into their own hands; their call to arms resulted in large numbers of men going north to join the insurgents. Two terrorist leaders joined them and under their leadership they put several Samaritan villages to the torch, as well as one toparchy capital. Tacitus records the incident and he emphasizes the negligence and corruption on the part of the procurator.[19] However, the allegations Cumanus had been bribed by the terrorists is not mentioned by Josephus, probably because it was more likely to be slander, for there is no reason to suppose he would have wished to whitewash the procurator.

Cumanus now had to act and sent six military units, reinforced by some Samaritan levies against the Jews' and Galileans' forces, in a single engagement and a great many were killed or captured. The Samaritans appealed to the legate of Syria, Quadratus, who found them guilty, he also ruled the actions taken by the Jews and Galileans was tantamount to revolt against Rome. He executed some of the Samaritans and all of Cumanus' Jewish prisoners and proceeded to uncover evidence of further rebellion, executed the leaders and then referred the whole matter to Rome. At this time, those rebels who had escaped Quadratus' *purge* now found they had increased their support and escaped to their strongholds from where they carried out a variety of attacks. Josephus points out in *JA* and *JW* that 'the whole of Judaea was now terrorized by raids from these brigands'.

Quadratus sent Cumanus to Rome to answer to the emperor Claudius. Accompanying him, in chains, were the High Priests Ananias and Jonathan, as well as the captain of the Temple. The acting governor of the province during his absence was Felix, who had been put in charge of Samaria when Cumanus had been withdrawn. In Rome, the intercession of the Jewish king, Agrippa II helped the Jewish case. The High Priests were exonerated and Jonathan requested Felix be made procurator of the province. This was granted and was unprecedented because Felix was a freedman, the fact he was Pallas' brother (one of Claudius' advisers, also a freedman) no doubt helped secure this appointment.

Josephus does not share Tacitus' dislike of Felix, who Tacitus describes as, 'brutal and licentious, behaving as a tyrant but showing the mentality of a slave'.[20] Neither does the picture of Felix we get from Acts compare favourably with Josephus' account, although it is probably correct to suggest the Acts version was designed to purposefully flatter Felix. The account that appears in Acts is taken from an account written by the accusers of St Paul to prejudice the procurator against the man who they considered a disruptive element. Josephus' account lies somewhere between the two, portraying Felix as inefficient rather than deliberately oppressive. According to Josephus, Felix's only transgression against the Law was his marriage to King Agrippa's younger sister Drusilla, after he had lured her away from her husband: a marriage that connected him to the Jewish royal family as well as indirectly to the imperial family.

Events in the province now appeared to have taken a different course and there was no longer a clearly visible distinction between the Jews versus Rome. With the rise of a nationalistic movement (which is usually associated with the followers of the Fourth Philosophy, however the various factions appear to have had very different agendas), there was growing dissatisfaction between opposing Jewish groups and coupled with the inability of Rome to control the situation plunged the province closer to disaster. Josephus commented on the upsurge in banditry and he noted that 'the country was going from bad to worse'.

Felix began by rounding up some of the terrorists and their sympathizers and crucified them. He sent Eleazar, the leader of the attack on the Samaritans, and several of his followers to Rome for trial. This only encouraged the terrorists to go underground; they took to assassinating their enemies at public festivals while mingling with the crowds. The first victim of the terrorists who were known as the *Sicarii* (dagger men) was the High Priest Jonathan. Josephus in *JA* says Felix was responsible for his assassination, having bribed Jonathan's friend to organize it, but the shorter account in *JW* says it was the spontaneous work of the *Sicarii*, which would seem a more reliable version, as Jonathan, a pro-Roman would have been a natural target for the *Sicarii*. By this time, the *Sicarii* were becoming the biggest threat to public order.

Along with the increase in banditry and political assassination, there also appeared on the scene a large number of militant prophets. Felix launched, with unnecessarily severe brutality, an assault on one charismatic leader and his followers (which incidentally included the apostle Paul), all of who were probably unarmed. Such acts as this led to the joining of political and military fanatics in a campaign of terror, estates of the wealthy were plundered and people were incited to revolt. Those who resisted found their villages fired or plundered as a warning to all who refused to join the anti-Roman campaign.

Josephus does not lay blame for any of the incidents on Felix, in fact he approves of the procurator's handling of the assault on the messianic figure of the 'Jew from Egypt' and his followers. However, Felix's insensitivity in handling affairs is seen in the disturbance at Caesarea, which was to play a large part in the contributing cause of the revolt a few years later. The Jews and Greeks in the city of Caesarea were in dispute, so Felix deliberately set his soldiers on the Jews. Josephus makes a point of saying the soldiers were local Gentiles and therefore natural enemies of the Caesarean Jews. Naturally, there were many Jewish deaths and much plundering. Once again Jewish notables tried to intervene with the usual result of a deputation representing both sides being sent to Rome.

Josephus may be suggesting in this account that the envoys sent to Rome voiced a widespread discontent rather than expressing concern over Felix's handling of a local matter. Whatever the case, Felix escaped punishment and was succeeded by Porcius Festus in AD 58/9, who held office for two years. Josephus has no complaints about him, he hardly mentions him in *JW*, except to say he rounded up some brigands.

In Jerusalem Festus supported King Agrippa who had a disagreement with the priests concerning a wall that blocked the view from the royal palace into the interior of the Temple. A Jewish embassy was sent to Rome under the leadership of Ishmael the High Priest but his attitude appeared hostile to Rome so he was replaced. Festus died during his term of office therefore his tenure was too short to have made any lasting impression. Before the arrival of the next governor, the High Priest Ananus, a Sadducee, tried to disperse the Christian sect and had James (brother of Jesus) put to death: this action was determined to be illegal and he too was deposed.

The year AD 62 heralded the period of the last two procurators of Judaea, and the prelude to revolt. Although Josephus' accounts become more animated at this point to show how wicked and evil these men were, he does, however, begin to omit vital information germane to the understanding of the initial cause of the revolt.

Josephus' account of the procurator Albinus (AD 62/4) in *JW* is at variance with his account in *JA*, no doubt partly due to the fact the two accounts were written at different times. In *JW* it appears Josephus is far too emotive to give an unbiased version because of his proximity to the events he is describing. In this version Josephus allows Albinus no redeeming features whatsoever. He tells us Albinus took advantage of his position to appropriate the property of private individuals and extort money under the guise of taxes. He also goes on to say he accepted bribes to release terrorists and gave free reign to the activities of the 'revolutionaries'. By comparison his account in *JA* portrays a man who bent every effort and made every provision to ensure peace in the land by exterminating most of the *Sicarii*, and who emerges from the narrative as a man unable to cope with the rapidly mounting unrest, finally submitting to a situation beyond his control.

There are two reasons why the account in *JA* is believed to be the more truthful version. First, the legate of Syria had not received any appeal from Judaea, which would have been the case had Albinus' behaviour warranted it. Second, Albinus was the only other procurator of the province to have been promoted to a more senior position, which Rome surely would not have sanctioned to judge by what happened to other procurators who had been disgraced.

Another explanation is that both of Josephus' accounts could be accurate. Albinus had been successful in his attempts to rid the province of the *Sicarii*, but his known cooperation with the High Priest, Ananus, gave the *Sicarii* a vehicle by which to exploit the situation. They attacked and kidnapped people within Ananus' circle to put pressure on Albinus to release other terrorist prisoners; Albinus was in a position where he was forced to act, seemingly in favour of terrorists within the province; the general consensus at the time that he had succumbed to bribery may have seemed correct, although his motives may have been misconstrued. The question is not which of the two accounts is correct, but what prompted Josephus to put a different emphasis on each one. The earlier version seems to incorporate the popular conception of the reasons for Albinus' behaviour, and no doubt useful for Josephus when trying to exonerate the subsequent behaviour of his countrymen to his gentile readers; it also served to exonerate Rome from blame by reference to the procurator's sole responsibility for events, something with which Rome would happily agree. In the later version in *JA*, Josephus gives a more balanced view perhaps when emotive issues of the conflict (Jew versus Gentile) was not of such paramount importance to his readers, and Josephus could afford to review the situation. Also in the later version he mentions the faction fighting that took place between the followers of the deposed High Priest, Yeshua b. Daneus, and those who opposed him. The importance of this anarchy in the city was obviously not considered relevant in the *War* narrative. What emerges from this account is that the terrorists no longer comprised the lower classes, for now armed gangs were emerging and the country was becoming divided into those who stood for law and order and Roman occupation and those who sided with the rebels.

However, accounts concerning the last procurator of Judaea are not so divergent, even Tacitus concurs with Josephus' comments on Gessius Florus, a man so wicked he made Albinus appear saintly. Josephus tells us there was no form of robbery or unjust punishment from which he abstained. Under his rule the situation rapidly deteriorated; Florus made no attempt to combat the terrorists who now virtually controlled the province.

Perhaps Florus was unable to restore order having only a limited military capability, but his oppressive and corrupt regime helped swell the ranks of the disaffected. Josephus gives no precise details of Florus' behaviour except for the part he played in the events that triggered the revolt. However, he does lay the blame for the revolt firmly on his shoulders: 'it was Florus who forced us to go to war'.[21] Not surprisingly given his attitude towards the procurators in general, the Roman historian Tacitus agrees: 'the Jews put up with the situation until the procuratorship of Gessius Florus, under him war broke out'.[22]

In AD 66, the legate of Syria, Cestius Gallus, realized that affairs in Judaea were far from satisfactory so he decided to pay the province a visit. Florus was not sent back to Rome, most probably because no specific charges had been made against him but Gallus did send a report to the emperor Nero impressing on him the gravity of the situation and the dissatisfaction the Jews felt towards Florus' procuratorship. Josephus implies Florus now deliberately worked to incite revolt in order to divert attention from him and prevent a direct appeal by the Jews to Rome. Nevertheless, there were other factors at play, those of an internal nature amongst the ruling class.

4

The Causes of Revolution According to Josephus (II)

INTERNAL DIVISIONS

*I warned them not to act recklessly and with such utter madness to expose
their country, their families and themselves to the direst perils.* (Life 19)

There is great emphasis placed by some scholars on the fact that from the outset
the revolt was led by the ruling class in order to keep their prominence within
Jewish society once Roman backing had been withdrawn, and who then tried to
establish themselves within an independent Jewish state.[1] The pivotal point came
when they refused to hand over the culprits who had insulted the procurator
Florus. These young men were the sons of notables and many references are cited
in Josephus' accounts to the young being at the forefront of dissent: 'The fathers
have eaten sour grapes and the children's teeth are set on edge'.[2] Within Judaea
there was little cohesion between the various Jewish factions, during the early
phases of the conflict the internal divisions amongst the various groups resulted
in civil war, first between the peace party and the insurgents and later between
the rival factions of the insurgents.[3] The Jews did not present a united front to
Rome until the final stages of the war.

The Jewish religious leaders did not as a whole support the war. After the
end of Herodian rule the High Priests had been entrusted with the leadership
of the nation and Josephus tells us that it was the High Priests who led the
'peace party'. Although Josephus recognizes the implications of civil strife he
is less illuminating about the actual nature of these divisions. He describes the
factions in various ways, bandits, extremists, terrorists and religious fanatics. The
implications are that this was a class struggle and this is generally accepted by
most scholars, one in particular takes this a stage further and uses four passages
from *JA* to demonstrate extensively this was not just a division between rich and
poor but a power struggle within the ruling class itself.[4]

However, there are problems interpreting Josephus' accounts. It is not clear
if he deliberately chooses to omit certain facts by covering them with a blanket
of generalities interpreted whichever way you choose, or whether the author
was blinded by his own role and prejudices of the situation he described. In *JW*
he clearly states the cause of the disaster came from within, 'since the blame lay

with no foreign nation'. In a number of texts Josephus emphasizes the guilt of the Jewish 'war party'. Also in *JW* he maintains it was the war party that forced peaceful inhabitants in the towns to revolt and he later states it was the same party that pushed for the suspension of the daily sacrifice for the emperor.

But who exactly comprised the war party? One scholar describes the emergence of a group, in essence Pharisaic, which he calls the Fourth Philosophy, a philosophy that 'sowed the seed from which sprang strife between factions and the slaughter of fellow citizens'.[5] This new philosophy instigated the waves of civil strife and murder so characteristic of the period. Josephus gives an account of its inception, stating it began under the auspices of Judas of Galilee and Saddok, with the rebellion of AD 6, 'the zeal that Judas and Saddok inspired in the younger elements meant the ruin of our cause'.[6] This party was more extreme than the Pharisees, for they displayed an irresistible passion for liberty and believed they should have no master but God. According to Josephus 'the folly that ensued began to afflict the nation after Gessius Florus'.[7] However, it may have been naive of Josephus to suggest this was the cause of the war with Rome. From this philosophy sprang the brigands and bandits Josephus speaks of.

However Josephus also considered the theological implications in this *innovation* in Jewish Philosophy, which he believed brought immediate consequences as well as chastisement from heaven, by its flouting of the precepts set out by Moses, as given in *Against Apion*, that provided the basis of a unified Jewish nation. Their innovation appears to be their equation of the Evil Kingdom of Daniel's prophecy with Rome and the end of days.[8] The theological implications weigh heavily with Josephus when he considered the actions and motives of the rebels, everything they did was coloured by his advocacy of the Law being the only source of harmony and transgression being punished by divine intervention. Josephus tells us little else about this Fourth Philosophy but we must accept originally it was in essence a religious rather than a political movement. He also says nothing tangible about the relationship of this philosophy with the Zealot movement or the *Sicarii*, which makes it difficult to reconstruct the relationship between the rebels of AD 6 and those of AD 66. He is also our only authority for the existence of the *Sicarii* who, it is believed, can be traced back to Judas of Galilee, inherited by his grandson, Menahem, and finally by their commander, a relative of Menahem, Eleazar b. Yair who led the final confrontation with Rome at Masada, where the philosophy of 'death before long dishonour' fitted well with the Fourth Philosophy's ideals (see Chapter 14 for a full account of the speech made by Eleazar). In this text however, the rebels under Eleazar b. Yair, are called Zealots by Josephus, which appears to indicate a link between the two groups.

On the other hand, it seems Josephus finds no real need to be precise in his attribution of specific events to specific factions, they are all transgressors therefore all come under the same general banner. When he was not using derogatory terminology to describe the rebels, then he used the terms, *Sicarii* and Zealot almost synonymously. If we assume that the *Sicarii* were the natural successors of the Fourth Philosophy, then who exactly were the Zealots and what connection did they have with both groups?

From Josephus' accounts a picture emerges of the revolt being led by the Zealots who were opposed to men of distinction, but he contradicts this in *JW* when he says members of notable families headed the Zealot movement.

> These leaders were Eleazar, son of Gion, the most influential man of the party, from his ability both in conceiving appropriate measures and in carrying them into effect, and a certain Zacharias, son of Amphicalleus, both being of priestly descent.[9]

This seems more plausible as only members of these families would have had access to the treasury to be able to issue the high quality coinage of the period. According to Josephus in *JW* the Zealots do not appear on the scene until the beginning of the conflict, they are the group against which the leading High Priests are attempting to incite the people of Jerusalem. In the absence of any further specific explanation from Josephus, various hypotheses have been put forward to explain who the Zealots were. Some say the Zealots came from within the ruling class, while others offer a more radical view.[10] According to them it appears the attack on the Zealots was due to the fact they were trying to form a new government not made up of the priestly aristocracy. It is believed the group, mentioned by Josephus in *JW* made up of several bands of brigands that entered the city and formed a coalition, were Zealots. Once inside the city these brigand bands attacked the High Priests and set about forming a new government. The hypothesis is that the Zealots comprised ordinary displaced persons, who fled to Jerusalem as their only recourse against Roman violence. He believes they had no connection with the Fourth Philosophy and were not a religious sect. It is more than feasible the Roman conquest provoked the formation of such brigand bands. Indeed it is possible such people swelled the ranks of the dissidents, but the subsequent organization and actions of this group suggest it was more than just a peasant's revolt. Also this theory does not reconcile how the original leaders of the revolt in Jerusalem, Eleazar b. Ananias and Simon b. Gamaliel, were allied with the Zealot movement or how they would have become leaders of bands of displaced people. It has been pointed out there is no great prominence of bandit leaders in the initial uprising, it would seem they took advantage of the situation, but were not responsible for it.

There is, however, another theory; that the word Zealot was a title, based on a Biblical verse from the book of Numbers adopted by those who followed the ideals of the Fourth Philosophy.

Josephus says Menahem, Judas' grandson, came to Jerusalem accompanied by armed Zealots and this statement is used to link the Zealots with the *Sicarii* and subsequently both groups to the Fourth Philosophy. The death of Menahem resulted in his followers returning to their stronghold at Masada, while the more moderate element remained in Jerusalem under the leadership of Eleazar b. Ananias who was a moderate revolutionary not a Zealot.

Therefore the *Sicarii* were the armed branch of the Zealots so the term *Sicarii* is a description not a title, which could have been applied to the extreme activist wing of the Zealot movement. However, there is one other source that may give clarification of who the *Sicarii* really were. In Acts (31.38) the term *Sicarii* is used in connection with the messianic figure of the Egyptian Jew, during the procuratorship of Felix, who descended on Jerusalem with 4,000 *Sicarii*. Surely it would be implausible that 4,000 armed dissidents accompanied this charismatic figure? The resulting massacre by Felix's troops suggests this was no armed uprising but that these people comprised ordinary followers of a specific doctrine. There is also another point to consider that the attitude of the *Sicarii* with regard to political assassination was basic to Zealot ideas rather than just the actions of an extremist wing.

The various leaders of the different factions have been designated by some in the following way; the Pro-Romans, which included King Agrippa and members of the High Priestly families; the moderate revolutionaries, those who were willing to come to terms with Rome, (Eleazar b. Ananias, Ananus and Josephus); the Nationalist element (Idumaeans, Simon b. Giora), these people were not called Zealots by Josephus and appear to have had their own socio/religious agenda; indeed it has been argued the preacher could be identified with the dissident leader mentioned in the Habbakuk *peser*, called the *Preacher of Lies*.[12] Those who adhered to the Fourth Philosophy increased their influence and following as the war progressed; the hard-core revolutionaries (Eleazar b. Yair) and finally the Zealot faction which had split in two, the *Sicarii* led by b.Yair plus the Jerusalem Zealots led by Eleazar b. Simon. As Simon held the military booty taken at Beth Horon he virtually held the reins of government. Later financial needs coupled with Eleazar's (b. Ananias) intrigues influenced the people to hand supreme command over to him. This hypothesis seems to be fairly accurate given the difficulties inherent in trying to reconstruct events solely from Josephus' narratives. It provides a link between the rebels of AD 6 and those of AD 66, and it also highlights the significant consequences of faction fighting within the ruling class in Jerusalem.

Both theories have points to commend them, however certain assumptions are made that cannot be substantiated. First, what if Josephus' words in *JA* are misrepresented:

> My reason for giving this brief account of it [Fourth Philosophy] is chiefly that the zeal which Judas and Saddok inspired in the younger element meant the ruin of our cause.[13]

...and he is not linking the Fourth Philosophy with *Sicarii* or Zealot, merely implying the idea of the Philosophy, i.e. no master but God, was carried to extremes by the later generation, for whom it became a political issue rather than a spiritual one? There is also, no tangible evidence to connect the members of Judas' family with the doctrine of the Fourth Philosophy, or indeed some inherited *messianic* tradition, other than their name, and certainly nothing to imply this Philosophy advocated violent resistance to Rome. It has been pointed out Judas' teaching of no master but God, gave a '*Jewish legal rationale for resistance to Rome*', but its concept was originally one of non-violent non-co-operation rather than violent extremism.

The implications are the Zealots and *Sicarii* were basically one and the same, the *Sicarii* being the armed wing of the extremist Zealots, is misleading, the *Sicarii* were carrying out political killings of Jews who sided with Rome, often being paid by members of the different elitist factions to do so. The Zealots, on the other hand appear to be members of the ruling class, the lower priests, who had the support of the populace and the help of the *Sicarii* under Menahem. But when Menahem tried to take over leadership of the revolt he was executed and his followers dispersed back to Masada, this does not imply they shared even the basic ideologies, so how is it possible they could have been the armed wing of the Zealot movement? Also, the fact that Menahem and his band infiltrated into the Temple by stealth shows that they were not invited to join the revolt by Eleazar.

Josephus' lack of information and ambiguous terminology also makes this aspect of the revolt difficult to decipher. The *Sicarii* do not appear to have been proactive before AD 44, neither do they take part in any of the major battles of the revolt or influence other revolutionary groups. The failed takeover bid for power by Menahem shows Josephus' claim that the Fourth Philosophy's heirs were solely responsible for the revolt is far from true. If we interpret the rest of Josephus' narratives correctly then the *Sicarii* were nothing more than hired assassins who would join whichever group was in the ascendancy. The Fourth Philosophy started in Galilee yet the revolt had not started there, nor in the countryside. It began in two urban centres Jerusalem and Caesarea, and it is apparent the common denominator was fighting between Jews and Gentiles, only then during the whole of the war, were the Jews actually united. Once they began fighting each other their purpose for doing so, of which there appear to have been many was lost.

In all there were five separate factions all with their own agendas, each one accused the other of bringing these events about and blurred the issue, each faction tried to justify its claims to lead a new independent Jewish state. It is possible that the most prominent feature of the revolt can be found in nationalism, and this can be traced back to the time of the Maccabees, however unlike that period of Jewish history, the Jews of the first revolt lacked unity. From the time of Herod the Great it appears that a duality was created between Jews and non-Jews as well as between Orthodox Jews and Hellenized Jews, resulting in the emergence of two separate nationalities.

What is apparent is that the war with Rome was running simultaneously with a civil war instigated by the collapse of the ruling class, which in turn opened the floodgates to dissident elements who had been waiting in the wings for just such an opportunity; this was not the first instance of civil war, for there had been one prior to this during the reign of Alexander Janneaus (103–76 BC). This opportunity could only have come about in such circumstances.

But was the collapse of the ruling class the underlying cause of the war with Rome or was it 'the occupying power and the nationalists reaction on one another, each provoking the other to further excesses until the final explosion came'?[14] That final explosion occurred in the town of Caesarea in May AD 66.

5

Insurrection: AD 65–66

From this date were sown in the city the seeds of its impending fall. (JW 2:276)

In April AD 65, before the legate Cestius Gallus' report on the procurator Gessius Florus could be acted upon, revolt was triggered by an incident involving the Jews of Caesarea Maritima, the provincial capital. The quarrel over civic rights was an old one and had flared up before in the 50s during the procuratorship of Felix. The quarrel mainly concerned the right of the Jewish community as a whole to have citizenship. The Jews had settled in Caesarea in large numbers as resident aliens, almost a parallel position to those Jews who lived in Alexandria. The Jews demanded they should take precedence over the Greek population, claiming the founder of the city Herod the Great was a Jew, therefore making Caesarea a Jewish city. This statement, despite being totally untrue, was also hypocritical, as the Jews had never accepted Herod as a Jew. Herod originally built the city as a model to Hellenistic (Greek) culture, therefore the city contained a large port and many Hellenistic civic buildings; to the south there was an amphitheatre and circus for chariot racing, as well as a great monument to his patron Caesar Augustus in whose honour the city had been named.

However, there were also underlying factors for the Jews' claims: the Jews of Caesarea were wealthier than the Greeks who lived there and no doubt felt they contributed greatly to the city's economic prosperity so consequently deserved citizenship so that they could gain control over municipal government. The Greeks, on the other hand were determined the Jews should remain *metics* (disenfranchised) as they rightly believed Caesarea had been founded as a gentile city; perhaps more importantly in their eyes, it was they who supplied the troops to Rome that kept the Jews in order.

Towards the end of Felix's procuratorship street fighting had broken out in the town. The local authorities did their best to punish those who instigated the trouble in an attempt to keep the peace, but this had the opposite effect, and Felix was forced to send troops against the Jews, for it was they who had initially caused the problem, finally getting them to capitulate.

Felix sent a delegation from both sides to Rome, which resulted with the emperor Nero deciding in favour of the Greeks. According to Josephus the Greek envoys bribed one of Nero's freedmen secretaries to make sure of a favourable result, and this may well be true. Nero confirmed the status quo of the Jews, they could still have individual citizenship but it would not be granted to them as a body. The Jews angered by this response returned home, determined to keep the quarrel alive, and Josephus explicitly cites their part in this continuing strife as *kindling the flames of war*. This long-standing quarrel finally erupted in an incident in AD 66 that Josephus believed triggered the revolt.

The synagogue in Caesarea had been built on land owned by a Greek. The Jews wished to purchase some extra land that adjoined their synagogue, the Greek refused to sell and then promptly started to build on it, in such a way that it blocked the front of the synagogue. A wealthy Jewish financier had offered Florus a bribe to officially restrain the building activities, which Florus accepted, but then did nothing more than instruct the commander of the cavalry unit in the city to keep an eye on the situation: effectively he left the two groups to sort it out. The following day was the Sabbath and when the Jews arrived at the synagogue they found some Greek youths sacrificing cockerels on the steps of the building. This act represented to the Jews a violation of the Torah (the Law as set out in the canonical books of the Bible), the synagogue and the Sabbath had been profaned and the Jews labelled *unclean* because the book of Leviticus specified this particular ritual for curing leprosy.

The inevitable riot ensued and the Jews, unprepared for battle fled, taking with them the scrolls of the Law. Thirteen of their leaders went to the city of Sebaste to appeal to Florus for help but he promptly had them arrested for having removed the scrolls, a completely incomprehensible action by the procurator. Perhaps Florus' pagan background had something to do with this, because the removal of a sacred object from a temple would represent to a pagan an evil portent for the city. The hostility continued to simmer in Caesarea before a final violent outburst occurred a few weeks later in Jerusalem.

Public anger in Jerusalem over the incident in Caesarea had been reaching boiling point so when Gessius Florus sent to Jerusalem requesting 17 talents (roughly 120,000 denarii) from the Temple treasury for 'Caesar's needs', saying he would come personally to Jerusalem to get it, he was met with hostility. Earlier, in AD 64, Agrippa and other leading members of the elite had decided to spend money from the Treasury on the construction of a pavement, which may have been in response to earlier appropriations of funds by greedy procurators, Agrippa anticipated similar occurrences in the future.[1] Some of the younger members of the Jewish ruling class found Florus' demand offensive and decided to ridicule him by holding a street collection for him. Indeed the perpetrators of the offence came from members of the ruling class. It is feasible that Eleazar b. Ananias' son was one of them, hence the reluctance to hand them over to Florus.[2]

Some of the malcontents railed on the procurator in the most opprobrious terms and carrying round a basket begged coppers for him as for an unfortunate destitute.[3]

Florus was outraged, but instead of going to Caesarea to deal with the trouble there, he arrived with a small force. A centurion, named Capito, with 50 men was sent ahead to clear the way. He entered the city and took up residence in the royal palace, the next day he convened a tribunal and called all the leading Jews of the Council (Sanhedrin) to demand they identify and arrest all those who had been involved in the collection so they could be punished; but the Sanhedrin refused, so Florus set his troops to sack the upper city. The soldiers looted extensively and took many prisoners, some of who were executed by crucifixion, amongst whom were Jews of Roman citizenship whose equestrian rank exempted them from that particular punishment. Queen Berenice, Agrippa's sister, who happened to be in Jerusalem at the time:

> witnessed with the liveliest emotion the outrages of the soldiers, and constantly sent her cavalry commanders and life guards to Florus to implore him to put a stop to the carnage. But he, regarding neither the number of the slain nor the exalted rank of his suppliant, but only the profit accruing from the plunder, turned a deaf ear to her prayers.[4]

The High Priests finally managed to quieten the situation and persuaded the populace to greet the two Roman cohorts despatched from Caesarea with civility as Florus had requested. Unfortunately the troops, on his orders, received their greeting in silence and when some of the more nationalistic elements in the crowd started calling abuse at Florus, the troops charged them; in the ensuing stampede many Jews were killed. As the cohorts attempted to advance through the city, heading towards the Antonia fortress, the Jews blocked the narrow streets with improvised barricades and took up positions on the flat roofs; from here they pelted the troops with a hail of missiles, mainly stones and tiles, until the troops were forced to take refuge in the palace on the western hill.

The Jews it seemed had won a victory: Florus was outnumbered and summoned the High Priests to the palace to inform them he was withdrawing to Caesarea leaving behind one of the newly arrived group of cohorts (500 men) to reinforce the regular garrison. These men were meant to represent imperial power but remained beleaguered in the palace, completely unable to patrol the streets and exert any imperial presence.

Florus, the Sanhedrin and Queen Berenice sent individual reports of the incident to Cestius Gallus. Gallus' emissary was despatched to Jamnia, where the Sanhedrin and High Priests had already gone to meet with King Agrippa. The whole group then proceeded to Jerusalem where Gallus' emissary inspected the scene of the riot, took note of the devastation caused by Florus' troops, sacrificed in the Temple as a goodwill gesture and then went back to Gallus to report the Jews were loyal to Rome but hostile only to Florus. However, by now the Jews had little confidence Gallus would act and have Florus sent back to Rome. They urged King Agrippa and the High Priests to send a delegation to the emperor Nero to complain. Agrippa was not happy with this course of action but realized if he denied the Jews their request then he risked open revolt.

Agrippa II's father, Herod Agrippa I (also known as Julius Marcus Agrippa) was the grandson of Herod the Great, and a spokesman of compromise. He had been brought up in Rome in the imperial household and succeeded in winning the favours of the emperors Caligula and his successor Claudius. In AD 37 Caligula gave him the lands that once belonged to Agrippa's uncle Philip, and when his other uncle Herod Antipas was deposed he was also given his lands. Agrippa intervened on behalf of the Jews when Caligula threatened to have the Temple desecrated with the erection of his statue.

He returned to Rome and was present when Caligula was assassinated in January AD 41; and played an important role as mediator between Claudius and the senate, helping Claudius become emperor. In gratitude Claudius bestowed Judaea and Samaria on him; this amounted to nearly all the lands originally held by his grandfather, Herod the Great. Agrippa now held the important city of Caesarea, and perhaps more importantly his descent from the Hasmoneans meant the Jews accepted him more readily as their king. He appeared to be a zealous Jew, offering sacrifice (as well as donating the golden chain given him by Caligula) to the Temple on his arrival in AD 41. His religious zeal was however, superficial for his attitude towards Judaism was a facade designed to appease his subjects; Agrippa was thoroughly Hellenized and in many respects behaved as a Hellenistic monarch. However his rule was short-lived and he died three years later. Claudius pronounced his 16-year-old son Agrippa II his successor but as he was still a minor, the emperor's advisers dissuaded Claudius from installing him on the throne. So, inevitably the province was reinstated and placed under procuratorial control. Nevertheless, the Roman government was obliged to offer the disinherited youth a kingdom. In AD 48 Agrippa II's uncle Herod of Chalcis died and he inherited this small independent kingdom that lay midway between Beirut and Damascus. He was also granted authority over the Temple, and had the right to appoint the High Priest.

Like his father, Agrippa II had been brought up and educated in Rome. It is possible he had remained in Rome until AD 53, when Claudius added the territories once ruled by his father's uncle Philip the Tetrarch to his realm; these territories ranged throughout the north and east of Palestine, including northern Transjordan, eastern Galilee, and on the death of Claudius, Nero added the city of Tiberias, the capital of Galilee and parts of Peraea.

Agrippa took up residencies in Jerusalem and Caesarea. In Jerusalem he enlarged the royal palace and renovated the Temple. In his own kingdom he re-founded the town of Panias (Caesarea Philippi), and renamed it Neronias after the emperor Nero, Claudius' successor. Herod Agrippa II was the most powerful Jew in Palestine. Although his territories did not include Judaea his influence there was great.

As already noted he had been on his way back from Alexandria when the trouble first broke out and he received a delegation from Jerusalem asking him to intervene in the affair. Agrippa knew the best course of action would be to make the Jews realize their grievance was not with Rome *per se* but with Florus. With his sister Berenice by his side he summoned a meeting in the gymnasium where he made an impassioned speech calling on all moderate Jews to rebuild the porticoes of the Antonia, (which they had destroyed in the recent outburst of violence), and pay their taxes, otherwise it would be tantamount to declaring war on Rome, a war they could not possibly hope to win. It is more than likely Josephus was amongst the multitude gathered to hear Agrippa's speech, which he reports in six pages of text, although it is unlikely he reproduced a verbatim account. The speech reflects the opinions of the upper-class Jews who favoured peace with Rome.

> when the Romans have won … they will make an example of you to other nations by burning down your holy city and destroying your entire race … not even if you survive will you find a place of refuge, since every people recognises the lordship of Rome.[5]

Agrippa further reasoned with them:

> You have not paid your tribute to the emperor and you have demolished the porticoes of the Antonia. You can only clear yourselves of the charges of rebellion if you rebuild the porticoes and pay your taxes. Florus does not own the fortress and Florus will not get your money

It appeared Agrippa made a favourable impression for everyone agreed to rebuild the Temple porticoes pulled down in the riot and to collect and pay the tribute to Rome, which amounted to 40 talents (approximately 282,325 denarii). However, when Agrippa repeatedly suggested they should obey Florus until another procurator could be sent to replace him the Jews remained adamant and demanded he be recalled and turning on Agrippa, hurling abuse as well as stones, hounding the king and his entourage out of Jerusalem. Despite his unceremonious exit Agrippa tried to put the Jews on a better footing with Rome by organizing the collection of the tax arrears from the rest of the country: however, the way was now paved for total confrontation with Rome.

There were two further events that heralded a complete break with Rome, the first was the occupation by rebel forces of the fortress of Masada, built by Herod the Great as his desert stronghold, and the second was the suspension of the daily sacrifice in the Temple for the emperor and his family. The Talmud mentions Zacariah, son of Amphicallus as the scholar, who at the outset of the revolt was responsible for the suspension of sacrifice; he was also a protagonist of the fundamental Zealot doctrine. Josephus however, ascribes the suspension of the sacrifice to Eleazar b. Ananias.[6]

Agrippa's unsuccessful attempts to persuade the mob, and his subsequent flight from Jerusalem split the Jewish ruling class in two, a small minority sided with the revolutionaries. Eleazar b. Ananias, who was from a High Priestly family and who held the post of Temple captain attempted to place himself at the head of the revolutionary movement. Eleazar persuaded the Temple officials to accept no more sacrifices from foreigners. This meant the daily sacrifices for the well-being of the emperor and his family would be abandoned, abolishing the imperial cult at Jerusalem; this act, for Josephus, was the foundation stone of the war with Rome.

The pro-Herodian party, the so-called 'peace party', was led by the ex High Priest, Ananias (Eleazar's father). Roman rule did not pose any serious threat to the Jewish religion, and the Jewish leaders, whether Pharisee or Sadducee, did not as a body support war with Rome. Ananias called a mass meeting in the Temple at the Court of Women to try to persuade the revolutionaries against this disastrous course of action, and to restore the daily sacrifice for the emperor. When the advice once again went unheeded they began to prepare for a counter revolutionary coup, as they realized that force would be the only way of curbing the rebels, with that in mind they appealed to Florus and Agrippa for military aid. They were still in control of the Upper City and looked to Agrippa and Florus to help oust the insurgents, led by Ananias' son Eleazar the captain of the Temple, who were in control of the Temple and the Lower City. Only Agrippa responded and sent two thousand cavalry, with whose aid the Herodians were able to keep control of the Upper City.

However, the revolutionaries led by Eleazar and his supporters, still held the Lower City, which included the Temple, which had now been turned into a citadel. The Romans remained in the Antonia fortress and Herod's palace. For seven days the two opposing forces confronted each other in a series of skirmishes but the Herodian forces were unable to gain any ground. Finally on the Feast of Wood Carrying (sometime around 14 August) the revolutionaries were joined by bands of pilgrims from the countryside including contingents of *Sicarii* and Zealots. Amongst these groups were agitators who saw this as more a social revolution, and hoped it would be instrumental in achieving economic reforms that would benefit the poor. The Herodian forces were now heavily outnumbered as renewed attacks on them began. Finally they withdrew to the royal palace with the revolutionaries in pursuit. Many Jewish nobles fled with the Herodian forces, some even took flight through underground sewers.

With the aid of the *Sicarii*, the revolutionaries set fire to the houses of Agrippa and Berenice, as well as the house of the High Priest, Ananias. The public archives where many debtors records were kept, was also put to the flames, a move apparently designed to win the support of the poor.

> The Jews in the Temple excluded their opponents from this ceremony, but along with some feebler folk numbers of the sicarii, so they call the brigands who carried a dagger in their bosom, forced their way in…they next carried their combustibles to the public archives eager to destroy the money lenders bonds and to prevent the recovery of debts, in order to win over a host of grateful debtors and to cause a rising of the poor against the rich, sure of impunity.[7]

The rebels had recognized the necessity of winning popular support to give them the power they needed to declare themselves the popular leaders of an independent nation. Meanwhile, Agrippa's troops, along with some of the Herodian nobles and defeated royalist soldiers had taken refuge in Herod's palace. The following day the rebels made an assault on the three massive towers of Herod's palace where the Roman cohort had taken refuge, situated by the north-west corner of Temple Mount, and massacred the entire Roman garrison; incidentally the massacre happened on the Sabbath, which in Josephus' eyes was a serious crime that would not go unpunished by God. It was a crime that would certainly not go unpunished by Rome.

Only the palace itself still remained in Herodian control, and the defenders managed to beat off the assaults of the revolutionaries, turning it into a siege. Menahem, the son of Judas of Galilee and his contingent of *Sicarii* arrived from Masada where they had infiltrated the fortress there, overwhelmed the garrison, broken open the armoury and equipped themselves with weapons; now they arrived in Jerusalem to assist with the siege. It appears that Menahem like his father Judas had messianic pretensions and expounded a somewhat extreme ideal of freedom. This group was the most committed of all the rebel factions and knew how to fight and organize a battle. When he arrived in Jerusalem, Josephus tells us, he was granted control over the attack on Herod's palace and the camp of cohorts left behind by Florus. Menahem and his men dug a mine beneath one of the towers along the outer wall, fired the props and watched as the whole structure collapsed. However, the defenders had built a second wall behind the tower, so there was no breach. Unfortunately, the defenders could not capitalize on this for they lacked sufficient numbers, and were by now tired and hungry. Their assailants had shown it would only be a matter of time before the palace would be taken.

On 6 September the Herodians sought terms with the revolutionaries. The king's troops and any other Jewish defenders were permitted to surrender and leave. However, their treatment of the Roman troops was very different, they refused them terms, so the Romans retreated to the three towers on the northern side of the palace, where they soon came under siege but they managed to hold out for a further 11 days, during which time the High Priest, Ananias had been found hiding in an aqueduct and was executed by Menahem. Finally in mid-September the cohort capitulated and agreed to surrender. In return for surrendering their arms they were promised safe conduct but as they were leaving they were massacred. The moderates now realized that Rome would definitely intervene to avenge the two massacres of their forces.

The struggle against the Herodian counter-revolution had resulted in a political shift, which manifested in political disunity. To the aristocratic nationalists the Zealot movement appeared menacing. Eleazar, the captain of the Temple who had taken power in May, now led the revolutionary government, which although anti-Roman and anti-Herodian, was a still a government comprised of property owners, who naturally feared a 'people's revolution'. They realized if Roman taxes could be abolished then the people might decide the same idea could be applied to paying rent, it would even be possible land could be redistributed amongst the poor; in fact a nationalistic revolution could easily turn into a social revolution.

The disunity amongst the rebel factions during the last days of the siege reached a climax with the murder of Menahem, who tried to usurp the leadership from Eleazar, whose father and uncle Menahem had murdered. Menahem and his group were taken by surprise and attacked in force on Temple Mount; some escaped the attack but were eventually tracked down, including Menahem who was tortured to death. Those of Menahem's supporters who managed to escape fled back to the desert stronghold of Masada under the leadership of Eleazar b. Yair, a relative of Menahem.

The successes of the rebels in Jerusalem was swiftly followed by further successful attacks upon Roman forces and two other Herodian fortresses fell into rebel hands; the Roman garrison at Cypros near Jericho was massacred, and the fortress of Machaerus, was evacuated by the Roman forces and settled by civilians: Josephus says this was in retaliation for the massacre at Caesarea.[8]

The breakdown of Roman authority now became the impetus for settling old scores in cities where tension had been greatest amongst the Greeks and Jews. Naturally, the violence once again began in Caesarea, where the Greeks slaughtered or expelled the entire Jewish population; according to Josephus this amounted to twenty thousand inhabitants, an act which Josephus sees as divine retribution on the Jews for their massacre of the Roman garrison.

Every decent citizen being terrified at the prospect of paying for the misdeeds of the insurgents.[9]

The reprisals were swift and Jews took revenge on Greek citizens in cities of the Decapolis and the Phoenician coast, which in turn led to counter reprisals against Jews in other Syrian cities. Conflicts and massacres spread throughout Syria and the violence extended as far as Alexandria in Egypt. Josephus tells us many Jews were forced to take up arms in self-defence and those who attempted to speak out against the massacres were annihilated. Everyone it seems was under threat; soon Palestine was split in two. Most of the big cities of the coast and the Decapolis remained Greek. Jerusalem, the Herodian fortresses and most of the small villages and towns of Galilee, Judaea, Peraea and Idumaea were in Jewish hands. The effect of this was to turn a minor revolt in Jerusalem, and conflict in Caesarea, from incidents in a small province to a major crisis in the eastern empire.

In *JW* (supplemented by references in *JA*), several paragraphs are devoted to a direct discussion of the main issues of the conflict, as Josephus saw it. The revolt was, for him, triggered by the following three incidents: Florus' attempts to obtain money from the Temple treasury which incited further unrest, and about which he did nothing, furthermore he exacerbated matters by marching on Jerusalem instead of trying to quell the unrest in Caesarea, thereby leaving 'a free field to sedition'. This in turn led to the abandonment of the daily sacrifice for the emperor and the provocation that set the course for full-scale war with Rome.

6

The March on Jerusalem

*Cestius, now that on all sides war was being made upon the Jews,
decided to remain inactive no longer.* (JW 2:499)

Josephus does not tell us if the legate of Syria, Cestius Gallus had contact with
Florus or any of the moderate elements in Jerusalem who had called for assistance.
Nevertheless Gallus had already assembled the XII legion plus 2,000 picked men
from the other legions, in Antioch. It was a considerable force consisting of over
30,000 men, made up of 12,000 Roman legionaries, 5,600 supporting Roman
troops and over 14,000 auxiliaries furnished by neighbouring Roman allies that
began the march on Jerusalem. Sometime in September the pro-Roman Agrippa
and two other client kings, Antiochus IV of Commagene and Sohaemus of Emesa
led their forces in person, consisting of archers and cavalry, and accompanied
Gallus to Ptolemais, the normal base for an invasion of Judaea.

From Ptolemais the Romans launched an attack against the border town of
Zebulon in the north-west of Galilee; the rebels, who were ill-equipped and
lacked military training were soon overrun, and fled to the hills, leaving behind
plentiful supplies which aided the invading troops. The Romans sacked the
town and began to lay waste to the surrounding countryside in order to starve
the Jewish peasants into surrender. At first everything went well and the army
had no trouble subjugating the small, unorganized Jewish settlements. After
overrunning the frontier district of Galilee, Gallus marched south and set up his
base in Caesarea.

Here the bulk of the army was stationed while a smaller force was sent ahead
to secure sea communications by capturing Joppa on the coast. The inhabitants
there had no time to flee and the Romans slew them all, according to Josephus
the victims numbered over 8,000 in total. Another force was sent to the area of
Narbatene, which bordered on Caesarea. Once again the troops ravaged the country,
killing the inhabitants, burning their villages and pillaging their property.

Cestius despatched Caesennius Gallus, the commander of the XII legion to deal
with Galilee. All the rebels in the region fled to the mountain, called Asamon, and
here Caesennius faced them in battle. While the rebels held a superior position they
easily beat off the attack killing roughly 2,000 troops. However, when the Romans
gained higher ground the rebels were quickly defeated, not being able to withstand

the charge of the heavily armoured infantry, and also were not able to outrun the cavalry. Most were killed although some managed to find a hiding place. The rest of Galilee was secured without too much trouble, mainly due to the fact the prosperous capital Sepphoris had taken a pro-Roman stance, and welcomed the legions. The other small towns and villages offered no resistance; a few extremists who had fled to the hills were eventually captured and summarily executed.

Caesennius then returned to Caesarea and rejoined Cestius and his troops. In mid-October Cestius Gallus marched towards Jerusalem, burning and looting as he went. At Lydda he razed the city to the ground, no doubt as a warning to the people of Jerusalem of the military strength that was seemingly about to descend on them. However, it was not all plain sailing for Gallus' forces; there was a hard pitched battle six miles (10 km) from the city that halted the army for three days. The Jews were not about to capitulate and when Gallus' force encamped at the top of the Beth Horon defile, they abandoned the Feast of Tabernacles, made a surprise attack and then penned the Romans in by occupying the heights that commanded the road at Gibeon.

After three days, Agrippa made a final appeal for peace by sending two emissaries to the rebels with an offer of free pardon from Gallus if they surrendered:

> But the insurgents fearing that the prospect of an amnesty would induce the whole multitude to go over to Agrippa, made a murderous assault upon his emissaries. Phoebus was slain before he had uttered a syllable; Borcius was wounded but succeeded in escaping. Any citizens who raised indignant protests were assailed with stones and clubs and driven from the town.[1]

Gallus noted the internal divisions amongst the Jews and saw this as a favourable opportunity for attack. He brought up the whole force, routed the enemy, and pursued them to Jerusalem. In the belief he could easily take the city, Gallus ignored the Jewish skirmishers and marched on. He established his camp a mile to the north of the city on Mt Scopus, confident the disunity inside Jerusalem would work in his favour. However, after three days there was no sign of surrender so Gallus occupied and burnt the suburb of Bezetha, which the inhabitants had abandoned, then he attacked the city walls in the vicinity of Herod's palace, where he encamped. Josephus says:

> Had he, at that moment, decided to force his way through the walls he would have captured the city forthwith, and the war would have been over.[2]

Five days later Gallus began an assault on the north wall of the Temple enclosure, then unexpectedly withdrew his forces to Mt Scopus and began to retreat to Caesarea. Josephus cannot give a valid reason for this sudden turn of events, which were unusual especially considering how close Gallus was to victory, the peace party were ready to open the gates to him, and the city would have been totally at his mercy: indeed his action seems inexplicable. The most tangible reason Josephus can offer is that Florus had bribed the camp prefect, Tyrannius Priscus, and most of the cavalry commanders, to dissuade Gallus from taking the city. This does seem to be a rather feeble explanation when clearly Gallus would presumably have had sound military reasons for his retreat; for example the purely military logistics of the lack of a siege train, or the onset of winter (for it was now early November, thereby curtailing the normal campaign season and impeding Roman success), for supplies would have been short). The fact these moderate factions, although they recognized the need for popular support, still sought to gain power by seeking Roman patronage, is apparent from the actions of Ananus b. Jonathan and others who tried to betray the city to Gallus.[3] There was also the danger of counter attacks from the rebels in the hills, and also the possibility that Gallus considered the offer to open the city gates was merely a trap. Perhaps Josephus wanted to look no further for a reason. For Josephus, being a Jew of Pharisaic origins, then the murder of the garrison, an act expressly against the Law, was an act which would incur the wrath of God and warrant divine retribution by prolonging the war and increasing the suffering of the Jews.[4] For had Gallus pursued this course of action and entered the city then, there can be little doubt the revolt would have collapsed.

Gallus was now faced with a difficult task, his communications with the coast were cut and as winter approached he had to find food for his army; he had no other recourse than to get back to Caesarea as quickly as possible. The nature of the terrain meant the Romans could not adopt the usual standard marching formation, for this would have strung the army out along many miles, in order to be secure they had to adopt the square column (*agmen quadratum*) a short, wide formation enabling units to turn into a battle line quickly, facing in any direction. The only drawback was that such a wide front slowed the army down, especially when travelling over difficult terrain.

Gallus' retreating forces were constantly harried by Jewish guerrillas under the leadership of Eleazar ben Simon, who had taken over leadership of the revolutionaries from Menahem. Militants from Jerusalem launched the first attacks at the rear guard of the column. The following day about a mile from the city Gallus was attacked from the hills by Jewish irregulars, equipped with javelins, slings and stones. The Romans were surrounded on three sides and any attempt at sorties up the slopes would result in them being cut off and destroyed. The stragglers who fell behind in the column were quickly despatched by Jewish forces. The situation gradually worsened and only when the baggage was abandoned did the Romans make any headway, managing to reach their old camp at Gibeon before nightfall.

Gallus remained at Gibeon for two days but because many of the baggage wagons had been abandoned, supplies were low. The Jews on the other hand were gaining strength as more reinforcements arrived to swell their ranks. Gallus ordered the draught and pack animals to be slaughtered, except for those that carried the ammunition and artillery, and the army set off again on 8 November. They travelled at first mainly through open country, which favoured the Romans, as it meant Jewish slingers and javelin throwers had to keep their distance. Finally, according to Josephus, they reached the narrow pass at Beth Horon where events took a turn for the worse.

The Jews had taken position at the top of the pass and had enough time to station men at the foot as well as on the precipices that hemmed the pass in on either side. When the Romans entered they found themselves encircled and were unable to operate on such a narrow front; the archers above easily picked off the soldiers. Josephus says:

> Cestius and his entire army were, indeed, within an ace of being captured; only the intervention of night enabled the Romans to find refuge in Beth Horon. The Jews occupied all the surrounding points and kept a lookout for their departure.[5]

However, the Romans secretly encamped the same night. Gallus selected 400 men to take positions on the roofs of the village and call out the watchwords to give the Jews the impression they were still there while the rest of the army made their escape along the road in complete silence, travelling approximately three and a half miles (5.6 km) before daybreak.

When the Jews realized the main force had escaped they overran and killed all the remaining defenders of Beth Horon before setting off in pursuit. Gallus now abandoned what remained of the baggage trains: it was not until they reached Antipatris they finally shook off their Jewish pursuers. It had been a complete military disaster for the Romans. The Jewish forces comprising mainly farmers armed with javelins and stones had completely routed the invincible fighting machine that was the Roman army. Roman losses amounted to roughly 6,000 men including at least three senior officers; they had lost armour and weapons, several batteries of artillery and an entire baggage-train of supplies to the rebel forces, this was no doubt the greatest Jewish victory for nearly 2,000 years.

> Antipas who had been besieged with them, in the royal palace and disdained to fly, was killed by the rebels. Cestius despatched Saul and his companions, at their request to Nero in Achaia, to inform him of the straits to which they were reduced, to lay upon Florus the responsibility for the war, for he hoped by exciting Nero's resentment against Florus to diminish the risk to himself.[6]

For the other factions who remained their task was one of organising a government that would lead them into war.

The defeat of Gallus meant any hope of negotiation with Rome was now lost, the Jews were now totally committed to war. The first task was to establish an independent government to oversee the necessary preparations for confrontation with Rome. The defeat and retreat of Gallus finally committed the Jews to all-out war. They now had a short respite before Roman reprisals would begin with a vengeance, many of the peace party now hastily abandoned Jerusalem. Some Herodian aristocrats who had stayed in Jerusalem, no doubt in the belief Rome would be victorious in crushing the resistance, chose this moment to flee.

> After the catastrophe of Cestius many distinguished Jews abandoned the city as swimmers deserted a sinking ship.[7]

This left the anti-Roman aristocrats, the High Priests, who still enjoyed a certain amount of prestige and influence with the people, who decided to bring the situation under their control and establish a democratic republic.

The Jews who had pursued Cestius, on their return to Jerusalem, partly by force, partly by persuasion brought over to their side those pro-Roman nobles who had remained in the city. They assembled in the Temple and appointed additional generals to conduct the war. Joseph b. Gorion and Ananus the High Priest were elected to govern affairs in the city. The constitution of the revolutionary government is ascertained from references in Josephus and Maccabees.[8] A council of state already existed in the Sanhedrin, which could be invested with additional executive powers. The popular assembly (which had existed during the time of the client kings but had been in abeyance during the Roman procuratorships), was now reconstituted as the ultimate authority, with the Temple court as its base.

It is at this point that Josephus refers to the followers of the prominent extremist Eleazar b. Simon as Zealots. It has been suggested:

> The absence of the term from Josephus' narratives before the end of AD 66 suggests that it was devised, or at any rate became generally current, only after the initial success of the rebels in purging the holy city of gentile troops. The Zealots, perhaps with religious considerations at first uppermost in their minds, seem to have been quite distinct from the faction of sicarii led by Menahem and his family, and to have been centred on Jerusalem, where in the fighting at the altar between the various factions they appear as quite a close knit and well defined sect.[9]

Both Eleazar b. Simon and Eleazar b. Ananias were overlooked for the post of supreme military commander, instead the council chose the High Priest Ananus

b. Ananus. He belonged to one of the elite High Priestly families in Jerusalem, his father and four brothers had all served as High Priest. Ananus also had held that position for only three months having been dismissed by King Agrippa and the Roman procurator. Alongside him were another High Priest, a High Priest's son and three other priests from noble families, they were styled 'generals' (*strategoi*). There were many secondary posts which may have gone to local leaders or token plebeians, which helped the aristocracy keep control of the situation while containing the popular mass movement by turning its leaders into officers and administrators of a new Jewish state organized along Hellenistic lines.[10]

Josephus says Ananus was of the anti-Roman party, but he was also aware of the problems confrontation with Rome could bring, so he hoped, by winning the confidence of the extremists, he would be able to turn the situation round and make them realize the futility of their aims and abandon their struggle. Ananus and another general appointed as his colleague controlled Jerusalem. The other general was Joseph b. Gorion who is mentioned only once by Josephus but not heard of again. He does not appear to be a significant figure and a year later Ananus has another colleague, Jesus b. Gamaliel. They ran affairs presumably with the help of other family members and allies, although we have no clear idea how this was accomplished. Control of Jerusalem was vital: the city held sway over the rest of the country and was of immense political and religious significance. Not only that but it was also the repository for the vast wealth of the Temple treasury.

One of the first tasks of the new government was the minting of coinage, a symbol of political independence, but it also served a practical purpose, to pay expenses. The new government struck three denominations of shekel in silver, the striking of which was a right denied by Rome to provinces. On the obverse the chalice was represented, depicting a branch with three pomegranates on the reverse. The rebel government continued striking these coins throughout the war, and were inscribed with a variety of cult objects symbolizing the Temple cult and dated from year 1 up to year 5.[11] The second task was to repair the unfinished north wall of Jerusalem; the ease with which Gallus had occupied Bezetha highlighted the significance of getting this work done as soon as possible. The long postponement of any Roman attack on the city meant they had three years to do the work. The wall was raised to over 10 metres (35 ft) in height, however the builders overlooked a section north of Herod's tower called Hippicus and failed to link the end of the new wall to the north-west angle of the old: this would later prove to be a very costly mistake.

The rest of the country was divided into eight districts under subordinate military governors. Apart from Jerusalem there was Peraea east of Jordan, one in Galilee together with Gamala, a fortress in the south-west corner of Agrippa's territory of Gaulanitis in the north, two in Idumaea in the south and three in

Judaea covering the approaches to the capital. The plan was to use the governors to establish a centralized control over the country and utilize the disparate militias as a regular army.

The various rebel factions also posed a problem as witnessed by the initial fighting against the Herodian party in Jerusalem during the month of August when Eleazar b. Ananias and his faction had killed Menaham. Ananus now marginalized the most popular of the faction leaders, Eleazar b. Simon who with his Zealot militia was the strongest faction by far. They had controlled Temple Mount and had taken command of the booty brought back from the victory at Beth Horon. Although Eleazar had been denied any prominent position within the new government thereby losing control of the public funds, his forces could not be dislodged from Temple Mount. Another of the popular leaders to fall was Simon b. Giora who had been a distinguished commander in the campaign against Gallus. He held the Roman spoils; money he had taken from Cestius, and a great part of the public treasure. Ben Giora's agenda was to instigate a programme of social revolution for the poor and he used his subordinate command to run a campaign of plundering against the wealthy estate owners. He was driven from his base in northern Judaea by government forces from Gerasa in the Decapolis but managed to flee to Masada where he carried on a similar campaign in Idumaea.

Other leaders who commanded only small forces were assimilated into the government administration. Three men were appointed to lead an attack on the coastal city of Ascalon, Silas the Babylonian, a deserter from Agrippa's army; Niger the Peraean, and John the Essene. Ascalon contained a garrison of two Roman auxiliary units which might have attacked the Jews from the rear while they were concentrating on a Roman attack from the north. However, the Jewish attack failed because it was ill-prepared and resulted in many Jewish casualties.

The government's policy was to enrol militiamen willing to accept the authority of military governors. They would receive payment, while new recruits were enrolled in the regular government units. Josephus gives us some idea how this worked when he describes the composition of the detachment sent by Jerusalem to Galilee under the command of Jesus b. Gamaliel. The detachment consisted of 600 men who received three months' pay in advance, plus 3,000 civic troops (*politai*) and 100 regulars (*hoplitai*). This is a good example of how the new government tried to create a formal army in the hope the military balance would shift against the independent militias and thereby curtail the threat to property and power posed by the various bands of armed revolutionaries.

Many men had joined one or other of these various military factions. They raided the houses of the rich and plundered estates to equip themselves with supplies and arms. However, the various military factions were undisciplined and uncoordinated.

The composition of many of the militia groups was fluid, with men coming and going or changing allegiances as the mood took them: each militia primarily owed allegiance to itself, its leaders and its own political, social or religious agenda. In effect the militias exercised a veto over the government, who lacked the necessary forces to be able to impose their will, therefore these independent units controlled practically all the country. It was basically a class conflict between the landed aristocratic classes and the mass of lower-class radicals. There was a war on two fronts, the struggle with Rome and the internal class struggle; this meant Judaea was in a very dangerous position as the threat of Roman invasion came ever closer.

7

Josephus in Galilee

They advised me to remain at my post and take precautions for Galilee. (Life 62)

The reasons for looking at events in Galilee as described by Josephus are twofold. First, this is where Josephus spent the initial period of the revolt in command of a vital military zone and about which he wrote two separate accounts one in *JW* and the other in *Life*. In fact these accounts differ so much that this has shed an unhealthy light on the veracity of his other works, especially *JW*. Second, do his accounts of the events in Galilee help us to understand what was happening in Jerusalem? And can we learn any more about the rebel factions to help clarify the causes of the war?

The two parallel versions of Josephus' time in Galilee are separated by a 20-year gap. *Life* contains more material about this period than *JW*, but where the two overlap there are many discrepancies, both in chronology and factual details. It is generally accepted *Life* was written to refute the accusations made against him by Justus, who claimed Josephus was responsible for the revolt at Tiberias. Justus of Tiberias was a local politician who after the war became Agrippa's secretary and an historian. Justus had reason to hate Josephus because he imprisoned him and his father.[1] Although others would argue against this, as the refutation made by Josephus is placed at the end of the work suggesting he was more concerned about the correctness of the war narrative as a whole, rather than trying to vindicate himself.[2] Some believe there is a possibility *Life* was written for those people who were intimately involved with the events of AD 66/7, i.e. Jews, although a pagan readership was not precluded.[3]

There are three main hypotheses concerning the reasons for the discrepancies in his two accounts. First, he made use of notes that he had taken during the war, which he applied more extensively in *Life*. Second, the passing years helped clarify those events, consequently he remembered more detail thereby adding or detracting from his account accordingly. Also he could have subsequently obtained additional information from others who had participated in the events described. Third, he deliberately avoided telling the truth. There is a possibility of a fourth option; that it could be a blend of all three, but taken overall *Life* is probably the more accurate account.[4]

After Gallus' defeat, most of the peace party had deserted Jerusalem, however

Josephus elected to stay. He tells us those who remained were 'persuaded' by the rebel faction; could it have been they were offered a tantalizing bribe? Josephus tells us he sought asylum in the inner court of the Temple, the fortress of the Antonia already being in their [rebel] hands. The inner court was occupied by Eleazar b. Ananias and his followers and they excluded anyone from their group who did not support their cause, therefore they must have believed Josephus was willing to give his approval for their actions. He, on the other hand, implies it was an act of prudence on his part, but his actual position is far from clear.

> In such obvious and imminent peril we professed to concur in their views, but suggested that they should make no move and leave the enemy alone if he advanced in order to gain the credit of resorting to arms only in self-defence. In doing so we had hopes that ere long Cestius [Gallus] would come up with a large army and quell the revolution.[5]

On the other hand he may well have acted in an ambiguous manner to avoid falling victim to one of two camps.[6] He rejoined the Pharisee moderates, led by Ananus, hoping Gallus would arrive and restore order. When Gallus was defeated, Josephus apparently threw in his lot with the rebels.

The rebel government set about making plans for the inevitable conflict that was to come with Rome. Needing to establish a command for the various military zones, generals were appointed from leaders of priestly descent. Surprisingly, Josephus was given the important command of the two Galilees. We can see from the account in *JW* the assembly who appointed him was convened not to provide leadership for the rebels, but to elect additional generals, implying the rebels already had generals leading them.[7]

Josephus gives two different versions about the nature of his command. In *JW* we are led to believe his duties were administrative, judicial and military, almost the same duties as a Roman procurator; clearly implying his mission was hostile to Rome. In *Life* he says he was sent to persuade the brigands to lay down their arms and ensure peace in Galilee. Does this mean Josephus had been entrusted to bring under his command all the disparate groups in the area? What is apparent however, is he showed little enthusiasm for the job he had been given and the implications certainly seem to point to the fact he was playing a waiting game.

It is possible that Josephus' statement to 'keep the peace' can be better interpreted if consideration is given to the fact there was much conflict between the cities in the north.[8] As well as continuing the usual Jewish/Greek tensions in the urban centres towns had now taken up arms against each other. If viewed in this way Josephus' statement does not necessarily reflect on his part a hostile attitude towards Rome but a need to unite the factions in a common cause.

Galilee was very different to Jerusalem in its political, social and economic organization. Galilee was 'an autonomous and self contained politico/ethical unit'[9] which had been administered by the Herodian tetrarch, Herod Antipas. Rome did not appear on the scene except between the years AD 44 and 66, even then the pro-Roman Agrippa II administered the region around Lake Tiberias. Economically, Galilee was a wealthy area, and appears to have been run on a patronal system,[10] however it was surrounded by hostile cities. Much of the land in Galilee was held by foreigners or absentee landlords, the peasants were crowded onto plots and were subjected to heavy taxes, tithes and debts. The best land was situated along the coast, in the Jezreel Valley, on the narrow plains around the Sea of Galilee, and in the south-western hills. To the east of Lake Tiberias were the lands of Agrippa II who was allied to Rome; Sepphoris the capital had already fallen to Rome and those who opposed Roman rule had taken to the hills.[11] When Jerusalem declared war on Rome, Galilee was undecided, but its proximity to the Syrian border meant the area was exposed to Roman attack; therefore it was vital Jerusalem exerted control over Galilee. So, it is a little baffling why they entrusted this important area to a pro-Roman priest, barely 30 years old with no military experience.

Perhaps the Jerusalem government was also playing a waiting game. Their action would certainly seem to indicate a half-hearted attitude to the war, perhaps they were hoping, by sending someone like Josephus they could still find a compromise with Rome, but the revolutionary turmoil into which Galilee was now plunged meant such a plan had little chance of success. Josephus had to establish his authority over an area where anarchy was fast gaining a foothold. The rivalries of the different classes, the individual Zealots and their followers, different cities with different attitudes, alternatively favourable and unfavourable towards Agrippa II meant that whether anti- or pro-Roman, even amongst themselves they could not agree. Josephus' narrative in *Life* certainly seems more subjective indicating he too was being thrown into the prevailing maelstrom.

Josephus faced two further problems; he had to associate with elements likely to assist in organizing the revolt, despite the fact he was against this course of action. Likewise, his affiliations in the region, especially to Agrippa II, as well as his own hereditary links with the royal house, meant Josephus now found himself in a singularly embarrassing position.

Josephus started his unifying mission by trying to win the local notables over to his side. He began by appointing a council of 70 over which he presided, the number of members including himself made a total of 71, the number prescribed by Jewish Law, so in effect this council became a local Sanhedrin. Each individual town had a governor and board of seven magistrates. He took great trouble to win the support of these local men thereby making it easier to control the region through them. Josephus relates how he organized the territories' defences, supervising the work himself and laying in supplies for future security. He surrounded the whole district with a series of defensible positions fortifying

Sepphoris, Tiberias, Tarichaeae and other smaller places. He says he also raised an army of 100,000 young men who he tried to train in the Roman way, although how and where he had acquired such knowledge he does not say. This was no easy task as he found many of the militias were unwilling to cooperate. According to one scholar the total number of Galileans armed and ready for conflict with Rome could not have exceeded 10,000 or so. Josephus and John of Gischala, the other leading figure in Galilee about whom more will be said later, could never count on more than 5,000 each and most of these men would have been bandits, men who were willing to fight for pay rather than any revolutionary zeal. Later, Josephus' troops would abandon him altogether:

> The troops under the command of Josephus, who were camping beside a town called Garis, not far from Sepphoris, discovering that the war was upon them, and that they might at any moment be attacked by the Romans, dispersed and fled, not only before any engagement, but before they had even seen their foes. Josephus was left with a few companions.[12]

According to Josephus the instructions he received from Jerusalem were imprecise, he was told he had to 'take precautions for Galilee'. It seems logical to surmise this meant to prepare for war and carry on rallying people to the defence of their cities, but perhaps Josephus intended to imply his instructions were imprecise so he could work to his own agenda, yet at the same time have an excuse if anything went wrong. Whatever the case his subsequent actions certainly give cause for questioning his motives. There were two specific incidents, one of which caused a severe rift between him and a prominent Galilean leader, John of Gischala. On both occasions he acted, supposedly, on religious grounds, i.e. that it was against the Law to steal, even from one's enemies, but in fact he acted in favour of Agrippa who was still allied to Rome.

What little we know of John ben Levi (known as John of Gischala) was written by Josephus, the man who was to become his sworn enemy. Although it seems John's origins may have been humble he did become a man of substance possibly through entrepreneurship in olive dealing, and certainly he was a prominent person in his hometown of Gischala in Upper Galilee. It appears the Hellenistic king Seleucus Nicanor (312–281 BC) had given special privileges to the Jews who were unwilling to use foreign oil, they were to receive a fixed sum of money from the gymnasiarchs to pay for their own kind of oil. John, according to Josephus:

> With the avowed object of protecting all the Jews of Syria from the use of oil not supplied by their own countrymen, [he] sought and obtained permission to deliver it to them at the frontier. He then brought up that commodity, paying Tyrian coin of the value of

four attic drachms for four amphora at the same price. As Galilee is a special home of the olive and the crop had been plentiful, John, enjoyed a monopoly, by sending large quantities to districts in want of it, amassed an immense sum of money.[13]

Josephus also tells us John had held a position of some importance in Gischala before the revolt, and that he became a leader of the local militia not necessarily from choice. It appears John was not a popular radical but Josephus saw the advantage of winning his allegiance and incorporating the Gischala militia of 400 men into the army; therefore John was left to organize the fortification of the town. However, it was not long before the two men clashed over control of the purloined imperial corn supply in Upper Galilee. According to Josephus John wished to sell it in order to rebuild the walls of his city. When Josephus demanded the supply be handed over to him John appealed to the two priests, who had accompanied Josephus, to give a ruling on the matter and they sided with John. Aware he had aroused John's suspicions he allowed him to continue, in what he believed was base dealing, in oil, even though he had accused John of profiteering.

A second incident occurred at Dabarittha when the wife of one of Agrippa's lieutenants was kidnapped. When the kidnappers asked to be given something from the plunder as their reward, Josephus refused, saying he was sending it to Jerusalem to help with the costs of reinforcing the ramparts. Instead he gave it secretly to those notables who were close friends of Agrippa.

But is the incident with the corn an admission of Josephus' treason? Purloining the corn supply would, without doubt, bring a swift reprisal from Rome and after all Josephus was supposed to unite the area and await, not create, open confrontation. Given his own beliefs and affiliations it seems his actions were half-hearted attempts to convince the people of Galilee he was seriously committed to the cause, without actually inciting open rebellion. But for those anti-Roman factions his actions, especially after the Dabarittha incident, would have seemed tantamount to treason.

On the other hand John's motives were very different. It was not that he craved wealth for its own sake, instead it seemed he craved the power such wealth gave. Indeed John's policy was to favour mass activity to defend the rebellion, and that included subordination of individual rights, especially rights of property to the common cause, while at the same time he demonstrated hostility to those whom he considered treacherous. This is the implication Josephus gives when he describes incidents that occured at Tarichaeae and Tiberias.

After receiving instructions from Jerusalem Josephus set about razing the palace of Herod the tetrarch, in Tiberias on the grounds it contained 'representations of living things' forbidden by Jewish Law: an action that mirrored the firing of the Hasmonean palace in Jerusalem, which had gained a great deal of popular support for the war party there; was this the reason for Josephus imitating this action? Tiberias was a major centre founded in the early first century AD by the client king Herod Agrippa and named after his patron the emperor Tiberius. The town was Hellenized in character even though the majority of the inhabitants were Jewish. Old rivalries and social tensions were brought to light by the revolution, and the city's mainly royalist ruling class was finding it difficult to maintain order. They were under threat from both the lower class and urban poor who were led by Jesus b. Sapphias, and from within their own ranks by Justus b. Pistus.

The anti-Roman faction were persuaded to join Josephus on his mission but before they could act were pre-empted by Jesus b. Sapphias and his men who took matters one step further and set fire to the palace, carrying off the treasures and purging the town of its Greek and royalist inhabitants. Josephus immediately went to Tiberias and seized as much booty as he could find which he then discreetly handed over to the pro-Roman notables with the intention (he says) of returning them to their rightful owner, Agrippa. This action was viewed with suspicion, after all Agrippa's army had been fighting the revolutionaries since the previous August, and it provoked a furious response in the nearby town of Tarichaeae.

We get some idea of his intentions with the speech he made at Tarichaeae:

> But as I saw citizens of Tarichaeae, that your city above all needed to be put in a state of defence and that it was in lack of funds to construct ramparts; as moreover, I feared that the people of Tiberias and of the other cities had their eyes on these spoils, I decided quietly to keep this money in order to encompass you with a wall. If this does not meet your approval, I am prepared to produce what was brought to me and leave you to plunder it; if on the contrary, I have consulted your best interest do not punish your benefactor.[14]

He had been denounced as a traitor and the town mob were yelling for blood, a frenzy being whipped up by both John and Jesus b. Sapphias, the governor of Tiberias at the time. Josephus' dramatic entrance into this lion's den caught everyone unawares and his eloquent speech, in which he said his intentions had been to use the spoils to build defences for the city, caused the Taricheans to express their approval, while the Tiberians heaped abuse on him. The result was that the various parties turned on each other and left him alone. It was a very clever way of manipulating events to secure his own self-preservation and all along this seems to be the sole aim of Josephus, finally culminating in the events at Jotapata. Josephus of course puts this animosity down to jealously on the part of his 'unworthy' rivals. However, from the two accounts Josephus supplies we may deduce this was far from the truth.

John of Gischala emerges from these narratives as Josephus' bitterest rival, and in *War* he is portrayed as a villain from the start. Josephus blames him for the revolt against him and an abusive but unspecified report of him follows. The portrait of John is one of a brigand who had mustered 400 men to plunder the villages of Galilee, yet Josephus' troops also consisted of bandits. By contrast, in *Life* John is said to have opposed the rebellion from the start and his aggressive actions were merely in defence of himself and his countrymen against attacks from neighbouring gentile cities:

> John son of Levi, observing that some of the citizens were highly elated by the revolt from Rome, tried to restrain them and urged them to maintain their allegiance ... a large force stormed and took Gischala ... Incensed at this outrage, John armed his followers and made a determined attack on the aforesaid people and defeated them.

He then rebuilt Gischala on a grander scale than before and fortified it with walls as a security for the future.[15]

The fact Josephus in *JW* sought John out and cooperated with him on his arrival in Galilee suggests he was a power to be reckoned with. Some scholars believe John was a person of considerable standing, not the rebel leader Josephus would have us believe from the accounts in *JW*.[16] Not only was he a wealthy landowner, but the future emperor Vespasian's son, Titus, had been prepared to negotiate with him as commander of Gischala.

The quarrel between them finally turned into open hostility and John in alliance with Jesus b. Sapphias (who Josephus maintains by pretending to be hesitant about entering the conflict was also really trying to get power for himself) and Justus (the man to whom his refutations are addressed in *Life*), attempted to raise Tiberias against Josephus. A failed assassination attempt on their part launched Josephus on a negative publicity campaign to discredit John and his supporters. They were offered a choice, either defect to Josephus or have their property burnt down. This telling passage suggests John's supporters were not all brigands otherwise they would not have owned property. By now Galilee was very close to civil war. John's militia abandoned the town and headed back to Gischala. Josephus captured the commissioners and they were despatched to Jerusalem to report the failure of their mission.

John had sent an appeal to Jerusalem for Josephus to be removed from his post, most probably on the grounds of treason, although Josephus likes to tell us either jealousy or bribery was the reason. Jerusalem listened, even the respected Pharisee Simon b. Gamaliel believed Josephus should be made to answer the accusations and a delegation was sent to remove him from office, by force if he would not willingly resign. Josephus' father warned him of the impending commission, and Josephus immediately took action. He transformed from a reluctant moderate to a militant almost overnight. The question is, why did he choose to remain in Galilee?

He says it was because the people wanted him to stay for fear they would be left without protection. However, there may be another motivation; rather than face the ignominy of being recalled he chose to create a diversion, just as he had done previously at Tarichaeae. He tells us that while he was at Asochis he had a prophetic dream telling him he would have to fight the Romans before he could achieve happiness. The next day Josephus mustered an army of 5,000 men and marched on Ptolemais (Acco) in an act of deliberate provocation to Rome. Josephus avoided meeting the delegation from Jerusalem and remained in Galilee until his capture, by Vespasian, at Jotapata.

John, on the other hand, had not perpetrated any act that would have been considered hostile to Rome. The reason John and Josephus had argued would appear to have been Josephus' unwillingness to commit himself to the war, but argues the idea is not as clear cut as it appears.[17] It is apparent John had gained the support of the moderate members of the Jerusalem government, who were hardly zealous to go to war with Rome, in his condemnation of Josephus' actions. Whatever those actions may have been it warranted serious attention from Jerusalem, Josephus as our only source for this period, is perhaps trying to create a different impression of events, and the motives he applies to John, of dishonest acts and banditry, should largely be ignored. John, unable to remove Josephus, and witnessing the destruction of Galilee by the Roman forces, finally fled to Jerusalem, where he joined the moderate party. It soon became apparent that Ananus and his followers had no real intention of going to war with Rome and were just waiting for an auspicious moment to affect a suitable surrender. John transferred his allegiance to the Zealots and became one of the great leaders of the revolt, remaining in Jerusalem until its destruction in AD 70.

Once again there may be another explanation for Josephus' attitude towards John's role in events. It could be, by inference only, that John was a member of Eleazar b. Ananias' faction, while Josephus was more closely allied with the ex-High Priest, Jesus b. Gamlas.[18] Both factions were united under the provisional government of Ananus. John had hoped for command in Galilee but when it was given over to the moderate's representative, Josephus, then every effort was made to remove him from office. The connection with Eleazar's faction was Simon b. Gamaliel, for it was at his behest the deputation was sent to recall Josephus: and it was Jesus b. Gamalas who sent warning, via Josephus' father, of the impending plot to remove him. If this were the case then Josephus' accusations of jealousy on the part of his rivals would clearly be justifiable. This hypothesis could also explain in some part Josephus' ambivalent behaviour towards John, as well as his (Josephus') motivation for remaining in Galilee. Both men were working to different agendas; Josephus was playing a waiting game, taking measures to fortify the cities in case of Roman attack but at the same time doing everything he could initially, to avoid a confrontation. On the other hand, John, shared the belief of Eleazar's faction, that conflict with Rome was inevitable, a question not of *if*, but *when*. Such subtle differences in motives would explain the attitude each man had towards the other.

However, Josephus' accounts do not clarify the situation. The differences that occur in the accounts can be ascribed to literary forms and the purpose served by the narratives.[19] For example, in *JW* Josephus is presenting his campaign to his advantage, whereas in *Life* it is used for self-defence. In fact there are few discrepancies that cannot be explained away by Josephus' shift of emphasis: 'If the *JW* shows what Josephus tried to make of things, the *Life* reveals how many obstacles stood in his way'.[20]

Although this theory may explain certain aspects of the narrative style of the ancient writer, it still leaves us with certain reservations about Josephus' honesty when dealing with events in which he played a prominent role. Can we really believe a man who was noted for his retentive memory, a trait not uncommon in the Jewish world, should have forgotten enough salient information to render his accounts so divergent? Even in modern times Orthodox Jewish boys learn by heart great portions of Talmudic literature and having a good memory is fundamental to their studies. This kind of memory training has been shown to increase the ability to recall accurately. The portrayal of John in *JW* as a brigand does nothing to enhance Josephus' reputation, it merely re-enforces the idea he wished to present the actions of the ruling classes (of which he was one) during the war in the best possible light to his readers. Understandably, given his beliefs, Josephus found himself in a unenviable situation but it seems he chose to remain in Galilee because he believed he had a destiny, which he later convinced himself was to tell the world about these events and redeem the greatness of his people. His subsequent actions, when viewed this way, can possibly be understood. At Jotapata his need was to survive at any cost, because he felt God had given him a sign in his dreams he had a mission to fulfil, although as with most divine invitations the *raison d'être* is not always made clear. Only if he truly believed this would he have been able to write about it in the way he does, because he sees himself as an instrument of divine will, rather than trying to justify his own behaviour.

What is evident from the account in *Life*, it is that both Galilee and Jerusalem had one thing in common, they were both disunited. Unlike Jerusalem however, Galilee had initially been less motivated to rebel against Rome. It seems the reasons for the Galileans joining the revolt stem directly from internal divisions and this may give us some clue to the causes of the revolt as a whole.

One plausible reason for the dissension can be found in the socio/economic breakdown of rural social relations.[21] It seems these socio/economic relations, in Judaea as a whole, were contractual, that is to say peasants were only bound to local landlords by contract.[22] However, it is possible in the case of Galilee there is evidence to show that here, at least the hypothesis is tenable.[23] The system utilized meant that wealthy and poor were bound to each other by ties of reciprocal obligation, i.e. patronage, a system employed in Mediterranean society overall. There is evidence to suggest this type of patronage meant landlords, such as John of Gischala, could rely upon the support of their clients in times of war.[24]

The problems originated with the urbanization of the Galilee area by Antipas, and the drainage of wealth due to the imposition of direct Roman rule led to absentee landlords,[25] the impoverishment of poorer farmers, and a partial collapse in the patronal system with the decline in relations between country landlords and their Roman/Herodian patrons; although Galilee was not as badly affected as some parts of the country. However, this gave some country landlords the opportunity to obtain more power, and in this respect we can clearly see from Josephus' accounts, the rise of John of Gischala as a wealthy country landlord and his influence over local peasants. So much so, he was able to retain the loyalty of his clients long after Galilee had fallen to Rome. Josephus also uses this patronal system to his own advantage as evidenced in *Life*.

> Wishing, moreover, under the guise of friendliness, to regain the Galilean authorities, some seventy in all, as hostages for the loyalty of the district, I made them my friends and companions in travel, took them as assessors to cases which I tried, and obtained their approbation of the sentences which I pronounced; endeavouring not to fail in justice through precipitate action and in these matters to keep clear of all bribery.[26]

A consequence of this partial breakdown of the patronal system was unemployment, landlessness and the subsequent development of large bands of brigands. Unemployment could also have been a significant factor in bringing about the revolt in Jerusalem, when the completion of the Temple threw a large number of men out of work in AD 64. Presumably the brigands that flocked into Jerusalem helped swell the ranks of the disaffected there and it seems clear whatever the machinations of the ruling classes, they still needed popular support. Jerusalem was an archetypal Oriental city divided between the ruling classes and the populace, and crowd protestations supposedly against the procurators could well have been directed against the ruling class.[27] The protestations usually occurred at festivals, especially Passover when the ranks of the urban populace were swelled by pilgrims and peasants from the countryside.[28] It could also be considered that the power of the disaffected mob may have contributed towards the actions of the rebel faction from the upper classes. Evidently, the social and economic changes in first-century AD Palestine produced conditions in part favourable to revolt.

Another salient feature of the narrative in *Life* is its singular lack of substantial references to Rome. On only two occasions does Josephus make any pertinent statements about what the Roman army was doing.[29] It is almost as though Rome was a hungry lion waiting to pick out the weakest from the herd, they were aware of its presence but were too busy establishing their own internal hierarchy to pay it serious attention. The evidence from the accounts in *JW* and *Life* help to clarify the nature of disunity amongst the Jewish people and Josephus, perhaps unwittingly, helps by his own attitudes to clarify the differences between the classes, which was a pivotal factor for the revolt beginning.

8

The Siege of Jotapata

Vespasian was impatient to make an end of Jotapata. (JW 3:141)

In May AD 67 Vespasian's army invaded Galilee. The size of the army, nearly 6,000 men, naturally provoked fear in the Jewish forces that were concentrated near Sepphoris, and who had no desire to encounter them in a conventional battle. The city of Sepphoris had already sent word to Vespasian asking for protection and he had furnished them with 1,000 cavalry and 6,000 infantry under the command of the tribune Placidus. The divisions made frequent assaults on the surrounding country causing a great deal of trouble to Josephus, now the commander of the Jewish army, and his men, so by way of retaliation Josephus attempted an assault on Sepphoris, but to no avail.

The Jewish army now began to disintegrate as men deserted and sought refuge in the fortified strongholds. Josephus had no other recourse than to fall back with his remaining forces to Tiberias, where his arrival filled the native Tiberians with alarm, as they realized he would not have fled there unless all hope of victory over Rome had been abandoned. Indeed Josephus was contemplating submission; he decided to write to Jerusalem explaining the serious nature of the threat he now faced.

> Neither exaggerating the strength of the enemy, which might subsequently lead to his being taunted with cowardice, nor underrating it, for fear of encouraging them to hold out when possibly inclined to repent.[1]

He requested them to either send more troops or to command him to negotiate with the Romans. While awaiting a reply, news arrived about the fate of the village of Gabara, which lay approximately 12 miles (19 km) inland from Ptolemais. The village had been completely wiped out by the Roman forces and all the inhabitants massacred; the nearby smaller settlements had also been attacked and destroyed and their people captured and taken into slavery. Vespasian's purpose was a deliberate policy to force the insurgents into battle or surrender. Despite the initial shock of this incident to the Jewish forces they still did not capitulate.

The key to the defence of Galilee lay in the small, fortified town of Jotapata, located on the north-western edge of Lower Galilee. It was a natural hill-top fortress protected on all sides and on the north by deep ravines. To the north was a round-topped hill that had been incorporated into the defences because it commanded the site. Beyond the hill and the northern defensive wall, the ground dipped away for about three-quarters of a mile (1.2 km) before rising again, providing a natural battleground for taking possession of the town.

Vespasian's tribune, Placidus had earlier attempted to take Jotapata and so make a name for himself in the process, and he expected to encounter little difficulty. However, forewarned of his approach the people of the town ambushed his force and managed to rout them, killing seven Romans in the process, while the Jewish losses only amounted to three men. Vespasian now decided Jotapata was the key to attaining submission of Galilee and sent engineers ahead to level the ground and widen the track. Josephus tells us that he had made Jotapata the most heavily fortified and garrisoned of all the strongholds and he left Tiberias and hastily made his way to Jotapata to join the remains of his troops to now take command. Placidus was sent with cavalry to set up a cordon on the hills around the town to prevent anyone escaping. The following day the main force arrived and set up camp to the north; a solid line of infantry and cavalry was dispersed round the town to establish a secure blockade, which cut off the defenders of Jotapata from the outside world. The fate of those who were inside was sealed, either they would have to capitulate or face a siege, which literally meant everyone inside the town, young and old, women and children would die or be enslaved. According to the historian Polybius the purpose of Roman massacre and enslavement in captured cities was to inspire terror and therefore affect an early surrender.[2]

The fighting began almost immediately. Vespasian used the fact he had a large army to intimidate the defenders of Jotapata who consisted mostly of peasants wielding nothing more than home-made weapons. This kind of physiological war-game would be advantageous if it succeeded because not only would it save the expense of a protracted siege but it would also give the Romans the advantage for their planned assault of the city of Jerusalem.

For five days Vespasian's army besieged the inhabitants of Jotapata with missiles and massed assaults by the heavy infantry, hoping this would weaken enemy morale. Josephus responded by sending out groups on sorties to surprise the Romans, who were ill-prepared for such tactics, and engage them in front of the walls. He reports only 17 Jews and 13 Romans were killed on the first day.

However, these tactics resulted in a stalemate; the Romans were unable to make any headway as they encountered heavy resistance from the Jews, and for their part the Jews could not risk open confrontation, being ill-equipped both in armour and weapons as well as lacking the necessary discipline of the Roman army.

Vespasian called off his attack and assembled a council of war. It was clear that Jotapata's defences were too strong for a frontal assault and it became obvious it would require siege warfare if the fortress were to be conquered. A platform of earth, timber and stone was constructed leading from the Roman lines up to the wall of the town. This was so that the dip could be filled and the ground levelled to enable the siege engines to be manoeuvred to the walls. Vespasian's army was put to work cutting down trees to make the framework for the platform, collecting stones to form revetments between the timbers, digging out the earth to provide the infill. This was no easy task and required a huge labour force. Vespasian had approximately 600,000 men and they needed to be fed. The necessary supplies have been estimated to have amounted to 900,000 gallons of water a day, and 300 tons of grain and fodder; this campaign was a costly exercise.

The Jews retaliated and mounted a defence to disrupt the siege works by shooting missiles and making several sorties to tear down the hurdles (the large row of protective screens that had been erected specifically to prevent such attacks), to attack the men working behind them, as well as breaking up sections of the platform and setting fire to the timber supports at night after the Romans had stopped work. In order to counter this threat Vespasian linked the hurdles together to make a continuous line along his front; the Jewish sorties now became too dangerous to risk and they were forced to remain behind the walls.

Finally, the siege works progressed unhindered and now posed a serious threat to the defenders of Jotapata. The platform would reach the height of the north wall and would enable the Roman assault forces to storm over the gangplanks on the narrow parapet opposite. Josephus ordered stonemasons to begin heightening the existing wall, and protected them by erecting screens of ox hide. They had to work night and day in relays in order to complete the task quickly, for time was of the essence. The wall was now almost 10 metres (33 ft) high with a new parapet on top, and towers spaced at intervals to allow them to fire at the attackers, who were now below them. Now it was Roman morale that was at low ebb as the Jews' confidence rose, they began once again to take the defensive with further sorties into enemy lines.

Vespasian was forced to change tactics yet again, and he abandoned the siege operations and began a passive blockade to weaken the Jews by starvation and thirst. Indeed water was a problem in the town although they were fairly well supplied with other provisions. There was no natural spring either on the southern ridge or the northern hill, so any water they had was kept held in rock cut cisterns, which filled with rainwater. However, May and June were months when hardly any rain fell, and the town was now swollen with refugees as well as the militia, so water soon began to be in short supply. The Jews had to go to the cisterns at the top of the northern hill to collect their daily ration, and often came under fire from the Romans. Indeed if the Romans had been able to continue their blockade the siege would have ended before too long.

However, Josephus formulated a plan and foiled the Romans. First he proposed to lead an outbreak from the town in order to obtain help from the rest of Galilee, the townspeople would not condone this possibly because they feared Josephus might abandon them. So, Josephus devised another ruse whereby the Romans would be fooled into thinking the town had enough water to withstand the siege. He arranged for several of his men to wash their garments and hang them on the walls to dry. When Vespasian saw this he naturally believed they had enough water, and the siege would be a protracted one, as he had no idea exactly how much water the cisterns contained, he decided to abandon the siege and resume his offensive strategy. The Jews also resumed their offensive and mounted fresh sorties against the Roman camp situated on the opposite rise.

Gradually the Roman platforms grew larger and the gap between the walls shortened. A battering ram was positioned to begin the assault on the wall, protected by archers and artillery who fired continuously at the enemy battlements above. The Jews retaliated with a heavy volley of missiles but Josephus saw that repeated blows on the same spot on the wall was rendering it on the verge of collapse. He devised another ingenious plan to paralyse the attack. He ordered sacks filled with rags to be let down by ropes to the place where the ram was battering, with the object of deflecting the ram and deadening the force by cushioning the blows. This seriously hampered the Romans for wherever they placed the ram the Jews followed and lowered the sacks, thereby protecting the wall from serious impact.

The Romans countered this by using long poles with scythes attached to the end with which they cut the cords supporting the sacks. As a last resort Josephus and his men had to consider firing the Roman defences. They gathered all the dry wood they could find and rushed out from three quarters of town and set fire to the engines, wicker shelters and props of the Roman earthworks. They were successful and the fire raged for an hour and consumed most of the Roman works. Men were also deployed on the battlements to rain missiles down on the Romans, Josephus tells us:

On one occasion one Jew who made his mark deserves record and remembrance; his name was Eleazar, son of Sameas, a native of Saba in Galilee. Lifting an enormous stone, he hurled it from the wall at the ram with such force that he broke off its head; then leaping from the ramparts Eleazar picked up the ram head and bore it with perfect composure to the foot of the ramparts. Now become a target for all his foes, and was receiving their hits in his defenceless body, he was pierced by five arrows. But without thought for these he scaled the wall and there stood conspicuous to all the admirers of his bravery; then writhing under his wounds he fell headlong with the ram's head in his hands.[3]

Josephus singles out two other men for bravery, the brothers Netiras and Phillip who dashed out along the lines of the X legion and charged the Romans, breaking their ranks and putting to flight all those they encountered.

Furthermore Josephus tells us that:

> Towards evening the Romans re-erected the ram and brought it up to the spot where the wall had been weakened by its previous blows. At this moment one of the defenders of the ramparts hit Vespasian with an arrow in the sole of the foot.[4]

The wound was superficial but it caused great consternation in the Roman camp, especially to Titus, Vespasian's son, who was first on the scene. Vespasian managed to rally himself and show them he was safe, which made them even more determined to fight the Jews more fiercely, and shouting encouragement to one another they rushed the ramparts.

The Jews despite being bombarded with a hail of missiles still held out on the battlements and continued to assault the Romans who were propelling the ram under cover of their wicker shelters. However the light from the fires they had set now assisted the Romans for it outlined the Jews against the darkness so the Romans could easily pick them off. The missiles continued to rain down upon the defenders until by morning the wall finally gave way and collapsed. Josephus gives us a glimpse of the power of these siege engines:

> [They] came with such force as to strike down whole files and whizzing stones hurled by the engines carried away the battlements and broke off the angles of the towers ... Some incidents of the night will give an idea of the power of this engine. One of the men standing on the wall had his head carried away by a single stone, and his skull was shot, as from a sling, to a distance of three furlongs [600 m].[5]

It has been suggested that Josephus may be exaggerating here, as the engine he describes is thought to be the *onager*, another form of stone projector not invented until later. The scene must have been a horrendous one, and Josephus tells us the whole of the surrounding area in the front of the fighting line ran with blood, and piles of corpses formed a path to the summit wall.

The following morning Vespasian launched his final assault. The breach in the wall was wide enough to allow his troops to force their way into the town. Vespasian deployed three units, made up from the cavalry, to clear an entrance, equipped with armour and levelled lances, while the main infantry supported them from behind. On either side of the main column the remainder of the army was drawn up, while the rest of the cavalry formed a cordon to prevent breakouts from the town, and lines of archers, slingers and artillery were deployed to bombard the town. Interspersed with these were heavy infantry units with ladders who would attempt to move under the cover of fire towards the undamaged parts of the wall to scale it, thereby drawing defenders away from the area of the breach.

Josephus left the manning of the intact portions of the wall to the fatigued or older men, placing the strongest at the area of the breach. He instructed his men to stop their ears when the Roman war cry came so not to be frightened by it; to crouch down and cover their bodies when the hail of missiles came and to fall back for a while, but as soon as the gangways were laid to spring onto them and confront the enemy. Josephus also:

> fearing that the wailing of the women might unman the combatants had them shut up in their houses, ordering them with threats to hold their peace.[6]

Before long the archers and slingers began their assault, and Josephus tells us there were so many missiles fired the sky darkened with them. As the defenders cowed beneath the barrage of rock and stone, the Roman column advanced down the platform towards the breach, the Jewish defenders sprang up and charged. The legionnaires formed a solid line across the platform, side-by-side, shield-by-shield in the *testudo* formation. The *testudo* or tortoise formation consisted of the men at the sides with their shields held vertically and locked together forming an unbroken wall, the men in the middle with shields held overhead formed a protective roof against projectiles hurled from above. They moved slowly in a shuffling methodical advance. Close-quarter fighting now ensued but the Jews had limited reserves whereas the Roman column was formed in great depth along the platform. The Jews were soon herded back and the Romans were poised to take the breach.

As the Romans approached the walls they were suddenly bombarded with streams of boiling oil, which penetrated the roof of the *testudo* on to the men beneath, penetrating their armour and scalding them. The centurions at the back quickly reformed into another *testudo* believing the oil supply would not last. They were correct but the Jews then hit the second *testudo* with a cold stew of fenugreek which covered the planks in a gluey slime, causing the soldiers to lose their footing and be trampled by the oncoming soldiers, either that or be impaled by missiles from the Jews situated above. There were no more advances by the Romans as fear spread through the assault column; Vespasian called off the attack, and Josephus and his men held Jotapata for another month.

The success of the Jews at Jotapata and the fact the bulk of Vespasian's army was tied up with the siege had the effect of spurring other fortified towns in Galilee to revolt. When the town of Japha revolted Vespasian despatched the commander of the X legion with a force of 2,000 infantry and 1,000 cavalry to quell it. The town was captured and most of the defenders slain, leaving only a few women and children who were taken into slavery.

At Jotapata the Romans began to work again on the platforms with the intention of raising them above the height of the walls, as well as constructing three timber-framed towers to protect the workers on the platforms and command the Jewish wall. The Roman archers could shoot down on to the Jewish battlements from above, which meant occupation of the battlements by the Jews became impossible. The only way the Jews could disrupt the work was by making frequent sorties, which were difficult owing to the towers' dominating position, and costly in terms of Jewish lives.

A deserter from the town offered Vespasian a glimpse into the defenders' position, and informed him that usually just before daybreak the exhausted men guarding the wall would fall asleep. Vespasian ordered his son Titus to take a small contingent of men and to raid the walls. On 1 July Titus and his men managed to stealthily climb to the parapet and despatched the sleeping guards. The Romans opened the gates and the soldiers waiting in reserve then surged forwards, they quickly secured the wall and overran the northern hill. The defenders had been caught off guard and panic swept through the town. Those defenders on the far side of the ridge could see no way of getting back to the town and committed suicide.

> They took refuge in one of the northern towers, where for some time they held their own; but, being surrounded by large numbers of the enemy, they at length surrendered and cheerfully extended their throats to their assailants.[7]

As the Romans advanced through the town, people fled in terror, some found refuge in the underground cisterns. The Romans killed all the men, and also some women and children, others were sold into slavery, finally Vespasian ordered the town to be demolished. In 1977 Israeli archaeologists discovered a mass grave here that included the remains of many juveniles (see Chapter 15 for fuller details).

Josephus had managed to hide in a deep pit, connected to a large cave that was not visible from above. A supply of provisions to last several days, and 40 other notables accompanied Josephus in his hideout. At night Josephus tells us he would emerge from hiding to try to find an escape route but was not successful. On day three the hiding place was eventually discovered by the Romans; Vespasian offered Josephus his life if he surrendered, and it appears that Josephus was willing to accept his offer.

Josephus relates the subsequent events in the cave and he tells how his companions preferred to commit suicide rather than fall into Roman hands. After haranguing his companions with a long rhetorical speech on the sinfulness of such an action (which failed to move them), he agreed to their suicide pact. He proposed the drawing of lots to decide the order of mutual killing. So, they drew lots; one-by-one they carried out the killing of their comrades until only Josephus and one other person were left. Josephus recounts with great pride his ingenious duping of his countrymen and makes it clear he 'had counted the numbers by cunning and thereby misled them all'. If Josephus had arranged the selection using a circular count then it has been proven that a clever manipulator could contrive the order in which to place themselves within the circle in order to survive.

Josephus and his companion gave themselves up and Josephus (for he says nothing more about his companion) was led away from the cave and escorted through a crowd of soldiers to Vespasian, Titus and other officers who were assembled to receive him. Josephus was spared death and was at first imprisoned ready to be despatched to Rome.

What happened next according to Josephus may seem a little incredulous to the modern reader. According to him when he was brought before Vespasian he addressed him with the words:

> You imagine Vespasian that in the person of Josephus you have taken a mere captive; but I come to you as a messenger of greater destinies. Had I not been sent on this errand by God, I knew the law of the Jews and how it becomes a general to die. To Nero do you send me? Why then? Think you that [Nero and] those who before your accession succeeded him will continue? You will be Caesar, Vespasian, you will be emperor, you and your son here. Bind me then yet more securely in chains and keep me for yourself; for you Caesar, are master not of me only, but of land and sea and the whole human race. For myself I ask to be punished by stricter custody, if I have dared to trifle with the words of God.[8]

Incidentally, the Roman historian Suetonius also reports the general prophecy of success made to Vespasian by a priest on Mount Carmel.[9]

At first Vespasian thought this was a ruse by Josephus to save his own life, but later changed his mind when he was informed of Josephus' prediction Jotapata would fall in 47 days, which had come true. Josephus, although still a prisoner was treated well by the future emperor and was to remain with him and his son Titus, with whom he developed a friendship for the remainder of the war.

There is an ambivalent attitude of Josephus regarding the suicide pact made by his comrades, and says that his narrative contains three quite distinct reasons for his rejection of this course of action.[10] One is moral, one practical and one relies on supernatural sanction. His rejection of the suicide pact on moral grounds is in stark contrast to the oration ascribed to Eleazar at Masada (see Chapter 14), where Josephus invokes standard Jewish practice: 'With us it is ordained that suicides should remain unburied until after sunset'.

It is strange that the episode in the cave does not appear in the same account of Jotapata in *Life*, but then in *JW* he was trying to exonerate himself from accusations of treachery. We therefore have to understand that this section of his narrative was written for the moderate Jews, and clearly it is with the aim of reinstating himself that he offers a series of explanations to those who would not be considered fanatics; the Zealots would never have agreed.

Jotapata had fallen at the beginning of July, which meant that there were still several months left in the campaigning season, enough time to wipe out any remaining resistance in Galilee. However, the demoralization amongst the Jewish forces caused by the fall of Jotapata had resulted in the virtual collapse of the resistance in Lower Galilee; only a few pockets remained, notably in Gischala in Upper Galilee in the north, and Tarichaeae and Tiberias on the Sea of Galilee, Mount Tabor inland and Gamala in the Golan Heights.

While the battle for Jotapata was raging Vespasian despatched the commander of the X legion, Trajan to Japha with 1,000 cavalry and 2,000 men. The town of Japha was situated in the vicinity of Jotapata, and encouraged by the uprising there, had also revolted. The town commandeered a strong geographical situation as well as being protected by a double ring of walls.

As Trajan approached, the inhabitants went out to meet him, as he saw, prepared for action, so he charged them, routed them and set off in pursuit. They burst into the first enclosure with the Romans in hot pursuit, but when they made their way to the second wall their fellow citizens shut them out fearing the Romans would also penetrate this area.

> Vainly did the swarming crowd batter the gates and implored the sentinels by name to let them in; while their supplications were on their lips they were butchered.[11]

According to Josephus the number of Jews slain was 12,000. Trajan sent word to Vespasian requesting him to send Titus to complete the victory. Titus was sent with reinforcements of 500 cavalry and 1,000 infantry. Titus commanded the right wing and soon his troops scaled the ramparts, and a desperate struggle ensued within walls where the defenders had rallied to meet the oncoming forces. The more able-bodied defenders clashed with the troops in the narrow alleyways while women pelted the troops from the roofs. The struggle lasted for six hours until the combatants were exterminated and the remainder of the population massacred.

The Samaritans did not escape either. The whole of Samaria was under garrison but the Samaritans had assembled on their sacred mountain, Gerizim and refused to move from the spot; their determined attitude appeared to be indicative of rebellion. Vespasian decided to anticipate their action so he sent Cerealis commander of the V legion with a force of 600 cavalry and 3,000 infantry. The commander then blockaded them on the summit, and due to thirst because of lack of water supplies and excessive heat, slowly the Samaritans began to descend the mountain whereupon the entire group were massacred.

Vespasian had marched back to Ptolemais to rest his troops before continuing operations in Galilee and established permanent bases for them in the non-Jewish cities of Caesarea and Scythopolis. The first and most important task was to restore sea communications. The rebels had reoccupied Joppa after Gallus' withdrawal and were using it as a base for piracy which not only endangered Vespasian's links with Greece and Italy but also the corn supply destined for Rome. A small force was sent to capture the port and establish a garrison, which was achieved with ease.

Caesarea was now the centre of operations as it was well placed for access to the north-east to Galilee and the Golan or south-east to Judaea and Jerusalem. The harbour meant that it could be well supplied and of course being a Hellenistic city was reasonably loyal to Rome. From here, Vespasian marched back across Galilee with a portion of his army to Caesarea Philippi in the Golan on the northern edge of Agrippa's territories.

King Agrippa solicited Vespasian's aid in bringing the client kingdoms back under his control, Tiberias and Tarichaeae were in rebel hands but there was strong pro-Roman feeling in Tiberias, where earlier in the year Josephus had intervened between the radical revolutionaries led by Jesus b. Sapphias and the Herodian supporters who wanted to make peace with the Roman forces. Titus was sent back to Caesarea to bring the remaining troops to Scythopolis, where Vespasian joined him and then from there they marched towards Tiberias establishing their camp a few miles outside the city.

Vespasian sent an officer to seek the town's surrender, this was responded to by Jesus b. Sapphias who led his forces out of Tiberias to attack the Romans. The royalists and other elites quickly defected to the Romans and the revolutionaries, losing what support they needed to defend the town, dispersed towards Tarichaeae a few miles north. The following day Tiberias opened the gates of the town and gladly welcomed the Roman forces. The battle for the Galilee had been won, the battle for Jerusalem was about to begin.

9

Final Conflict in Galilee

Galilee was thus now wholly subdued after affording a strenuous training for the impending Jerusalem campaign. (JW 4:120)

The rebels in Tarichaeae grew stronger than ever as fresh militiamen arrived to make a stand against Rome. Josephus had fortified the town with a circuit of walls and on the waterfront the rebels had assembled a flotilla of boats, which could be used to effect an escape should their land operations fail. Vespasian and his army were camped just south of the town where they erected stout defences.

> While the Romans were entrenching their camp, Jesus and his companions, undeterred by the strength and orderly discipline of the enemy, made a sally, and at the first onset dispersed the workmen and pulled down a portion of the structure.
>
> However when they saw the legionaries mustering, they hastily fell back upon their own party, before sustaining any loss; the Romans pursued and drove them to their ships. Putting out into the lake just far enough to leave the Romans within bowshot, they then cast anchor and, closing up their vessels one against another like an army in line of battle, they kept up as it were a sea fight with their enemy on shore.[1]

Vespasian countered this attack by stationing 2,000 archers, under the command of Antonius Silo, on a hill close by the town. The Jews had also amassed a large force on the plain, so a cavalry unit comprising 600 men was sent to deal with them, under the command of Titus. However, he found the number of Jews facing him prodigious and so sent word back to Vespasian requesting more men. Trajan, one of Vespasian's officers, joined him with a further 400 cavalry. Titus' force charged the Jews who did not flee immediately, but against such odds these lightly armed men stood little chance. Many did make it back to the town but Titus pressed home his advantage and re-formed his cavalry leading them through the edge of the lake so to be able to pass round the end of the wall. The Romans finally broke into the town and proceeded with the onslaught. Jesus and some of his followers managed to escape and fled across country, the rest of the townspeople were either slain or taken into slavery.

Vespasian ordered a cordon to be placed around the town to prevent any more rebels from escaping; he also had rafts constructed so that his troops could pursue those who had tried to escape by boat. At the western edge of the Sea of Galilee a naval battle ensued. Josephus describes the boats as 'small built for piracy and weak in comparison with the Roman rafts', they were presumably fishing boats commandeered by Jesus. The Roman archers quickly mowed down the Jews who lacked armour, in contrast to the Romans who were protected from Jewish missiles. The rafts soon overwhelmed the small boats and the inmates were either hacked down by javelins or thrown into the water, where they met a similar fate: the waiting soldiers killed those who managed to struggle ashore. The devastation was complete and Josephus tells us 'the beaches were thick with wrecks and swollen bodies, which hot and steaming in the sun made the air foul'.[2]

Vespasian separated the townspeople into the citizens, Agrippa's subjects, who had been caught up in the events, and the non-resident insurgents. The city and its citizens were handed back to Agrippa, while the others were taken to Tiberias, where Vespasian divided them into various categories. Six thousand of the strongest young men were sent to work as slaves on the Corinth canal, the remaining were sold to slave dealers, those who were either too old to work or had some other disability, perhaps numbering as many as 1,000 in total, were killed.

Only three of Josephus' strongholds still held out against Rome, all of them were located in northern Palestine; Gischala, Gamala and Mount Tabor. Vespasian now headed towards Gamala, a fortress in the south-west corner of Agrippa's territory of Gaulanitis, which had been kept forcibly loyal to the king by a garrison of his troops. The town was perched on a spur of the Golan Heights described by Josephus as being: 'hung in the air and on the point of tumbling on top of itself from its very steepness'.[3]

This garrisoning of Gamala had prevented the rest of Gaulanitis, which contained a large Jewish population, from joining the national cause. Agrippa had unwisely withdrawn his garrison forces and was forced to conduct a siege lasting seven months in order to put the fortress out of action as an effective rebel base. The defenders, which included refugees mainly from Galilee including both rebels and villagers from the vicinity, had held out admirably, which gives some indication of the town's strength.

However Vespasian was determined that Gamala should be taken and he deployed three legions, the XV on the north side, the V in the centre and the X to the south. All three legions were ordered to construct siege platforms to create a level approach. As usual the defenders attempted to disrupt the operations but were out-shot by the Roman artillery. King Agrippa approached the ramparts and tried to parley with the Jews and get them to capitulate. The reply he received was a slingshot which hit him just above his right elbow.

Before long the siege platforms were completed and battering rams were brought in which quickly made breaches in the wall. The legionaries broke

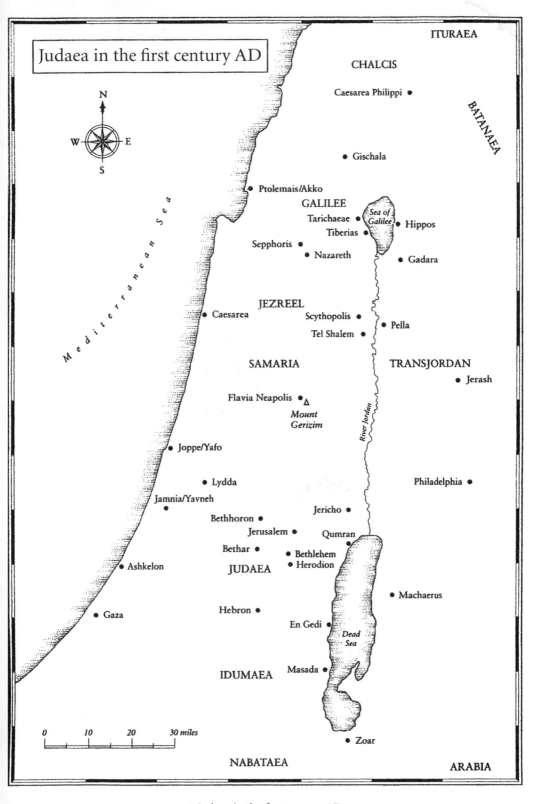

1. Judaea in the first century AD

2. Roman siege camp at the foot of Masada

3. Roman ballista stones found at Masada

4. Hill fortress of Masada

5. Model of the Temple at Jerusalem in 1st Century AD

6. Model of Jerusalem in 1st Century AD

7. The Wailing Wall – all that remains of the Second Temple

8. Herodium – aerial view

9. Herodium – one of the fortresses built by Herod and occupied by the rebels

10. Inscription recording Pontius Pilate at Caesarea

11. Caesarea

12. Qumran, where the Dead Sea Scrolls were found

13. Emperor Vespasian

into the town and the defenders made their way towards the ridge at the top, which had the desired effect of drawing the soldiers deep into the narrow streets involving them in house-to-house fighting, one of the most difficult of all types of combat because the enemy can be over, behind, or on either side. Given this situation there was no opportunity to deploy the natural disciplined mass of the Roman fighting machine effectively. The legions were broken into smaller groups therefore unable to rely on support; after a sudden attack from above the forward ranks of the legions panicked and turned to flee, only to find their way blocked by their comrades coming through the narrow alleyways behind them. In the panic to escape the troops climbed onto the roofs on either side; the weight of the men cause the roofs to collapse as well as the floors beneath.

The Jews then pressed home their advantage by raining down missiles on to the stampeding troops below. They also began to slaughter those men who were trapped in the wreckage of the collapsed buildings. The emperor Vespasian was among the mass of soldiers having joined in on the attack, he found himself isolated near the ridge with a small group of soldiers. Luckily they did not waiver; they formed a shield wall to protect themselves from the missiles hurled by the Jews in front of them, and slowly made a withdrawal. Most of the remaining legionaries were able to make their way to the breaches in the wall and back to Roman lines.

This defeat was indeed an inglorious one for the Romans and left Vespasian's troops demoralized. Vespasian set them to work to raise the platforms higher, and tried to encourage them by making a speech, in which he told them:

'Fortune flits back again to one side. You have slain myriads of Jews, but yourselves have paid but a trifling contribution to the deity.'[4]

His words seemed to animate his troops.

The inhabitants of Gamala were naturally delighted with their success over the Romans. However their elation slowly began to turn to despondency as they realized any chance they had of escaping was virtually nil and they were running out of supplies. They faced a blockade, and soon hunger and tiredness would also become their enemy. Nevertheless they continued to take what precautions they could, the bravest amongst them manned the breaches; the rest manned what remained of the wall. However, when the Romans began strengthening their earthworks to attempt a fresh assault the people of the town began to flee down the ravines or through underground passages.

While the people of Gamala were suffering Vespasian undertook a minor diversion by dispelling the occupants of Mount Tabor. Mount Tabor lay midway between the Great Plain and Scythopolis. The citadel was surrounded by a wall, erected by Josephus, and adequately supplied with provisions including water.

Vespasian despatched his general Placidus with 600 cavalry. Finding the ascent of the mountain impracticable Placidus made peaceful overtures to the crowd who had fled there, and offered terms. The crowd responded favourably and began to descend, however, their real agenda was to attack the Romans. Placidus feigned flight and in doing so led the Jews out on to the Plain; then suddenly he wheeled his cavalry round and routed them. The majority of the Jews were slain, the remainder were captured, and the masses still remaining on the mountain were given promises of protection, so they surrendered Mount Tabor to Placidus.

In Gamala some inhabitants were making their escape, others were dying of famine while the bravest were still attempting to withhold the siege. On 9 November, about a month into the siege, three soldiers of the XV legion crept up to the base of the projecting tower of the town and began to undermine it. As it was still dark the sentries positioned above did not see them so they could carry out their work unhindered. The soldiers succeeded in rolling away the five chief foundation stones then leapt out of the way; the tower came toppling down. The guards at the other posts fled, and the Romans cut down many who tried to escape. The people in the town were in a state of panic believing the Romans had burst in, however the Romans did not effect an entry until the following day.

Vespasian's son Titus who had not been present at the initial attack now returned and he led 200 dismounted cavalry and some infantry and entered the town quietly. The guards were surprised and ran through the town where general panic ensued: Josephus describes the scene vividly

> Some snatching up their children and dragging their wives after them, fled with their wailing and weeping families up to the citadel; those who faced Titus were incessantly dropping; while any who were debarred from escape to the heights fell in their bewilderment into the hands of the Roman sentries. On all sides was heard the never ending moan of the dying, and the whole city was deluged with blood pouring down the slopes.[5]

Vespasian led the main force through the eastern wall, the mass of Jewish fighters along with their families had gathered on the steep rocky crag that overlooked the town. As the Romans began to haul themselves up the slope the Jews rained down missiles upon them. However, a fierce wind began to blow, it was so strong it almost blew some of the defenders off the crag, and sent their missiles wide of their targets. The Romans pressed on, and it became clear to the Jewish defenders there was little hope, the Romans had them encircled on the whole of the lower slope, advancing towards the summit and slaughtering everyone in their path. Some brave defenders continued to fight, but resistance became futile as the Romans pressed home their advance.

What happened next is the stuff of legends and has caused scholars to refer to the site as the Masada of the Golan.[6] Some scholars were under the impression that a mass suicide had occurred here as it had done at the desert fortress of Masada much later in AD 73, when a band of Zealots made one last stand against the might of Rome (see Chapter 14). According to Josephus, the people on the crag knowing defeat was inevitable plunged over the precipice to their deaths. According to him 4,000 had been slain by the Romans but 5,000 actually committed suicide; men, women and their children.

In a recent publication a more pragmatic approach has been taken to this story.[7] The site of Gamala has been under archaeological investigation since the 1990s and it appears the only place along the crest of the ridge where there is a vertical cliff high enough for someone falling off it to die with any certainty is at the summit, which today can only accommodate a few hundred people at most. In antiquity it may have been larger but not by very much:

> even if we accept 500 people standing on the ridge it would be physically impossible for all but a few to reach the summit and jump headlong to their deaths. The rest would not have made it. The remainder of the ridge on the north slopes down, indeed, to the gorge below.[8]

It has also been suggested that while the mass suicide at Masada most probably did occur because there the people had time to listen to the impassioned speech of their leader Eleazar ben Yair, no such time would have been afforded to the people of Gamala. The truth must be that the remaining defenders and townspeople were trying to flee down the steep northern slope in panic, with the inevitable result that many were trampled underfoot and died. Some of the more agile may actually have reached the gorge and safety. However, according to Josephus only two women survived, the nieces of Phillip son of Jacimus, a distinguished man who had been commander-in-chief to Herod Agrippa.

In the 14 seasons of excavation at Gamala no human skeleton was ever uncovered. This is due no doubt to the fact of the supreme importance of Jewish religious command for burial of the dead. The Romans would no doubt have allowed burials to take place. The dead were probably buried in a mass grave somewhere in or near the city; the recent discovery of a mass burial cistern at Yodefat [Jotapata] confirms this hypothesis, so it will be a matter of chance if burials are discovered at Gamala.

The defeat of Galilee was almost complete, only Gischala remained. The legions were now despatched to their winter quarters at Caesarea and Scythopolis; so Vespasian sent Titus with 1,000 cavalry on a special mission to destroy the last rebel outpost in the region. Josephus tells us that the inhabitants of Gischala were inclined to be peaceful consisting of mainly agricultural labourers, but he says they had been affected by numerous gangs of bandits and incited to rebel by John of Gischala.

John's position appeared hopeless, for Gischala was now isolated and could not call upon any assistance. The town's defences were weak and could be taken easily, instead Titus chose to blockade the town because winter was approaching, they would soon have starved to death.

> Titus, on riding up to Gischala saw that the town might easily be carried by assault. But he knew that were it taken by storm a general massacre of the population by his troops would ensue; he was already satiated by slaughter and pitied the masses ... he therefore preferred to induce the town to capitulate.[9]

When Titus arrived he offered terms and then withdrew allowing the Jews on religious grounds to give their response after the Sabbath. John's plan was to evacuate the town and march south to aid the defence of Jerusalem, Vespasian's final objective, and for which he was busily training his troops in their winter camps. John outwitted Titus by using the excuse of the Sabbath to buy him time to effect an escape. Titus' mistake was to not put a cordon round the town to prevent such an event.

During the night John and his militia slipped out of the town and set off for Jerusalem, the non-combatants, mainly women and children, followed them; naturally many could not keep up the pace of the forced march. They called after their husbands, begging them not to desert them but John's orders prevailed. Josephus tells us what John supposedly said to his militia: 'Save yourselves and flee where you can and have your revenge on the Romans for those who are caught'.[10]

The next day Titus came to the walls of Gischala to conclude the treaty. The people who came out and hailed him as a benefactor and liberator of their people opened the gates to him. They told him of John's flight and begged for mercy, telling him to punish those insurgents who still remained. Titus immediately despatched a squadron of cavalry in pursuit of John and his men. However, they failed to catch up with him, and he made good his escape to Jerusalem, however many of his companions did not share his good fortune and were massacred at the hands of the Romans, according to Josephus they killed about 6,000 and rounded up and brought back 3,000 women and children.

Meanwhile Titus entered the city and had his troops pull down a portion of the wall in token of its capture. He did not attempt to punish those accused of being insurgents instead he threatened them, believing this was the best course of action as he had no proof of their guilt except for the accusations of others. He garrisoned the town before his departure and returned with his troops to their winter camps where they were to be prepared for the final battle of the war, the capture of Jerusalem.

However, Jerusalem was in the future; Roman strategy was continuing to reduce the military strongholds and armed bands of revolutionaries that still existed throughout the rest of the country. The successful campaigns of Vespasian and Titus ensured the north and west had been subdued. Attention was also given to the east and south-east (Peraea and Idumaea), to reduce all pockets of resistance down to a small area of Judaea that surrounded the capital, Jerusalem.

By this time Samaria and the Sharon Plain had also been secured. The Samaritans also had a tradition of revolution against the foreign oppressors, and could well have joined the Jews in their rebellion, however by the first century AD, the divisions between the two bordered on communal hatred. Nevertheless the Samaritans had also suffered under Roman imperialism and Samaritan peasants faced the same problems as their Jewish counterparts. In AD 36 an armed crowd assembled at Mount Gerizim, their holy sanctuary, under the leadership of a Samaritan messiah to challenge the authority of the Roman procurator.

A similar situation occurred again during the siege of Jotapata. Vespasian was sent word that the Samaritans were gathering at Mount Gerizim, and naturally he feared they were on the verge of rebellion. He sent the commander of the V legion with 3,000 soldiers and 600 cavalry to deal with the situation. The Samaritans were taken by surprise and barricaded themselves upon the top of their mountain, without food or water. By 27 June many had deserted through lack of supplies, and when the defenders were sufficiently reduced in numbers the Romans began their ascent, storming the position they massacred everyone. From this point onwards Samaria abandoned any revolutionary ideas, and Roman domination went unchallenged in the area.

A similar situation occurred in the Sharon Plain where there were large Jewish communities. Early in the autumn of AD 66 the Greeks had terrorized the Jews with massacres both at Caesarea and Ascalon, followed shortly afterwards by the storming of the city of Joppa by Roman troops, who killed the defenders and burnt the city to the ground.

The earlier victory over the Romans at Beth Horon (see Chapter 4) had given fresh hope to the revolutionary movement and Ananus, and his council in Jerusalem sent a force to Ascalon. A small troop, roughly 500 men, and a small contingent of cavalry were the town's only defence. The Jews had hoped for a surprise attack but the Romans were ready and waiting, they rode out on to the plain to meet their attackers, as Josephus describes:

> When raw levies were confronted by veteran troops infantry by cavalry undisciplined individuals by regulars who fought as one, men with nondescript weapons by fully

armed legionaries, men guided by passion rather than by reason by men who instantly responded to every signal, the issue could never be in doubt.[11]

The Jews were badly defeated and lost two of their commanders in the battle. Nevertheless, the Jews did not give up and tried a second time to take the city, this time the Roman commander had set ambushes in the passes on the road down into the plain, once again the Jews were routed by Roman cavalry attacks.

However, the city of Joppa, situated on the coast, was taken by the rebels and used as a major base for their activities in the plain of Sharon. In AD 67 as the Romans made further incursions into the country many rebels fled to Joppa. The Jews busied themselves building a fleet to keep themselves supplied and also to harass Roman shipping: before long Jewish pirates were attacking Egyptian and Syrian trade routes as well.

After the siege of Jotapata, Vespasian sent a troop of soldiers and cavalry to take the city. The Romans managed to enter the city at night for surprisingly the walls had been left unguarded. The Jewish defenders set out in their ships and were waiting just off the coast. It was unfortunate a sudden gale blew up and because Joppa had no natural harbour, but consisted of a rugged shoreline the force of the north wind dashed the ships against each other or on to the rocks. Most of the crews perished either by drowning, or being crushed in the wreckage, or if they managed to struggle ashore hacked down by the waiting Roman forces as they made their way on to the beach. The city was garrisoned and the surrounding villages plundered or destroyed.

Tenaciously the rebels still held out in some areas of the plain. Josephus tells us after the conquest of Galilee Vespasian still had to capture Jamnia and Azotus before Jewish resistance was finally wiped out in the Plain of Sharon. The territory now held by the rebels was almost half, they were effective only in Judaea, Perea and Idumaea, and here were surrounded by Roman forces to the north and west. To all intents and purposes the stage was now set for the final assault on Jerusalem.

10

Civil War in Judaea

Can any still dread the war with the foreigner and foes who are by comparison far more lenient to us than our own people. (JW 4:183)

When John entered Jerusalem he and his men were surrounded by crowds of people desperate for news of what was happening in Galilee. The rebels declared the Romans had not defeated them rather they had decided not to waste valuable manpower fighting a lost cause but decided to come to Jerusalem to defend the city and fight them on safer ground. It would have stupid and reckless they said to risk their lives for Gischala when they could defend the metropolis. However, when the people heard about the massacres that had taken place they became very alarmed and started to fear the inevitable Roman advance upon the capital.

John, according to Josephus, began to incite various groups by raising their hopes and making out the Romans were not as strong as everyone believed, telling them how the Roman army would have great difficulty in surmounting the walls of Jerusalem considering their difficulties in subduing Galilee: 'By these harangues most of the youth were seduced into his service and incited to war'.[1]

However, there were many who could foresee what a final confrontation with Rome would do to the city and its inhabitants and wanted to make peace. Therefore the city's population soon became divided between those who sought peace and those who sought war. It was not just the population of Jerusalem who were wracked by these divisions, party strife had broken out throughout the whole country. Civil war now ensued, turning brother against brother, with whole families being torn in two by the conflict of interests. Various groups of individuals intent on war with Rome began to emerge, and they roamed the countryside pillaging their neighbours, before banding together and beginning to pillage the rest of the country until there was no difference between their actions and that of the Romans, which Josephus seems to imply, was the lesser of the two evils.

Finally these 'bands of outlaws' as Josephus refers to them, having joined forces headed towards the capital. It was a religious obligation that all Jews could find refuge in the city and as the city had no commander, there was no one to stop these disaffected groups from entering. Supplies were short, and the added numbers only made the situation in Jerusalem worse. The gangs soon began to make sorties outside the city to raid and rob, but more importantly so Josephus tells us, began to commit murder, especially of eminent citizens.

It was now inevitable the rebels attempted to try to seize power for themselves; they elected their own men into the High Priesthood and caused strife between the official authorities in order to engender a split between them. The leader of the rebel contingent was Eleazar b. Simon, he and his Zealot militia had been entrenched upon Temple Mount since the previous autumn. With the arrival of John and his Galilean forces and the populace's rising anger against the aristocratic regime's incompetence he took the opportunity to go on the offensive.

They deposed the High Priest, Matthias ben Theophilos, and instituted a new more democratic procedure for election to this post. In the past the High Priest had been chosen by the king, Herod Agrippa, and later by Roman governors from amongst the elite Sadducean families. The rebels then informed the populace that they would now carry out the selection for the High Priesthood by lot, as according to them this was the ancient custom prior to Roman occupation.

They summoned one of the High Priest clans called Eniachin, and cast lots, from all its eligible members, for the position of High Priest. An individual called Phanni, son of Samuel was elected. He was from a small village and had no connection whatsoever with any priestly descent indeed he was according to Josephus, 'such a clown that he scarcely knew what the high priesthood meant'. They had the poor man brought to Jerusalem, dressed him in ceremonial robes and gave him instructions how to act. It seems the rebels thought this was highly amusing but the other priests: 'watching from a distance, beholding the mockery of the law, could not restrain their tears and bemoaned the degradation of the sacred honours'.[2]

According to Josephus, the final outrage performed by the rebels was the slaying or imprisonment of members of notable families. One of their first victims was Antipas, a member of the royal family, who was in charge of the public treasury. They arrested and imprisoned him; Levias one of the nobles, and Syphas, both of royal blood, the latter a person of high reputation throughout the country, followed in similar fashion. The population of the city was now thrown into dire panic. The rebels realized by keeping their prisoners alive they ran the risk of their captives' families avenging them and attempting their escape, so they decided to have them assassinated and employed John, son of Dorcas to carry out the deed. John and ten others entered the gaol and butchered the prisoners. To cover their actions they made it known the prisoners had been colluding with the Romans and therefore had been slain as traitors.

Men such as Gorion b. Joseph and Simeon b. Gamaliel, by speeches to the assembly and private visits to individuals, urged the council to take action. They were supported in their efforts by the most eminent of the High Priests, Jesus

b. Gamlas and Ananus b. Ananus. Ananus the senior of the chief priests finally decided to take their advice and instigated an insurrection of the populace.[3] Immediately the rebels converted the Temple into their fortress and refuge from the outbreak of popular violence about to descend upon them. Ananus called his supporters together and urged an armed assault upon the rebel Zealots to drive them from Temple Mount.

While Ananus was enlisting men, probably from the aristocratic youth, the Zealots hearing of the impending assault left Temple Mount and instigated their own assault in the Tyropoeon Valley, between the Lower and Upper City, the same area that had been involved in the Herodian coup of AD 66. Fighting broke out in all parts of the city with a mutual discharge of stones, followed by long-range javelin combat, and finally hand-to-hand sword fighting, which resulted in great slaughter. Wounded civilians were taken into the houses by their relatives while those Zealots who were wounded made their way back to the Temple. Through grim determination the ill-equipped populace won the day and managed to push the Zealots back through the gates of the Sanctuary, across the Outer Court and into the Temple itself.

The Zealots barricaded themselves in and remained secure from further attack, however, they were not completely cut off from the rest of the city, now surrounded by government soldiers. Ananus did not think it right to make an assault on the Temple and so had selected 6,000 armed men to guard the porticoes, who took it in rote to do the duty.

This was just the beginning of an internal revolution that would shake the city to its foundations. While the battle with the Zealots had been taking place the other militias had stood aside. It could possibly have been because they wished to ascertain the final outcome before they made their stand. It would have been to their advantage to see the Zealots crushed, as they were their main rivals to power. However, Ananus now sent a delegation to Vespasian inviting him to come and take over the city. Ananus had already made his feelings clear in the speech he made to the crowd:

> Is it not lamentable that, while the Romans never violated one of our scared usages ..., persons born in this very country, nurtured under our institutions and calling themselves Jews should freely perambulate our holy places ... Indeed if one must nicely fit the phrase to the fact, it is the Romans who may well be found to have been the upholders of our laws, while their enemies were within the walls.[4]

Elite Jews, like Ananus and Josephus, although in the minority had hoped they would be able to contain the popular movements while at the same time win battles throughout the rest of the country. By doing so they would have been able to negotiate a peace with Rome and possibly reinstate a client king, like Herod

Agrippa. However, the internal revolution divided the aristocracy and their plan to seek peace with Rome was now untenable. They faced either annihilation at the hands of the popular revolutionaries or Roman rule, and for them the latter seemed preferable.

Josephus tells us that John of Gischala was personally responsible for the collapse of Ananus' party. He says John accompanied Ananus on his rounds pretending to side with the cause, then he would slip away at night to the Zealot camp and tell them all he had learnt:

> Seeking to escape suspicion, he displayed unbounded servility to Ananus and the heads of the popular party, but this obsequiousness had the reverse effect; for his extravagant flatteries only brought more suspicion upon him, and his ubiquitous and uninvited presence produced the impression that he was betraying secrets.[5]

John was bound over by oath and swore he would be true to the people, and not betray their plans. Believing him Ananus now admitted him without further suspicion and even went as far as to make him their delegate to the Zealots to arrange a treaty because they were anxious to preserve the Temple from further pollution. John is quoted by Josephus as making the following speech to the Zealots:

> Often I have risked my life on your behalf to keep you fully informed of all the secret schemes devised against you by Ananus and his followers; but now I am exposing myself to the greatest of perils, in which you will all be involved, unless some providential aid intervene to avert it. For Ananus impatient of delay has prevailed on the people to send an embassy to Vespasian inviting him to come at once and take possession of the city.[6]

He then further incited them by telling them Ananus was offering them terms only to trap them into leaving the Temple, once outside they would be set upon by the guards. He urged them to seek external aid, although from where he did not specify, though according to Josephus, it would come from the Idumaeans.

The Zealot leaders Eleazar b. Gion and Zacharias, both of priestly descent having decided to summon aid from the Idumaeans drafted a letter to the effect that Ananus was about to betray them to Rome. They sent two messengers with the letter who were instructed to speak eloquently on behalf of the Zealot cause. The Idumaeans were ready to join forces and sent 20,000 men to march on Jerusalem under the command of four generals John, James b. Sosas, Simon b. Thaceas and Phineas b. Clusoth.

When this army approached Jerusalem Ananus shut the gates and mounted guards upon the walls. He tried to parley with them and sent Jesus the next in line to the High Priesthood to the tower opposite to speak to them. This proved to be of no avail as the Idumaeans were unwilling to lay down their arms or turn against the Zealots. The gates remained locked, denying them the right all Jews had to enter the city, and they spent the night weathering a torrential storm outside the walls with only their shields to cover them from the rain.

Josephus says this storm was a portent, and one can imagine that a good number of the population would have viewed it in a similar way, he says: 'Such a convulsion of the very fabric of the universe clearly foretokened destruction for mankind, and the conjecture was natural that these were portents of no trifling calamity'.[7]

The signs were viewed as a message from God who was angry with the Idumaeans for bearing arms against His Holy city, and one can imagine that Ananus and his party also believed God had intervened to win the battle for them. However, it was not only the Idumaeans who were suffering the effects of the torrential storm; many of the guards on duty along the walls also sought refuge in their own homes, or in the towers or colonnades.

The Zealots tried to find a way to help their allies. A group of them left their comrades and made their way across the Outer Court. They sawed through the gates of the Sanctuary and made their way across the city to the wall opposite the Idumaean camp; the Idumaeans at first supposed they were under attack and the men were Ananus' troops. The gates of the city were opened and the Idumaeans flooded through. Their first act was to free the Zealots taken into custody, then they made their way to Temple Mount where they attacked the soldiers who were guarding the colonnade. Josephus tells us by dawn there were 8,500 dead; although how reliable this figure is we cannot say.

The Idumaeans and their Zealot allies now turned their attention upon the rest of the city, looting every house and killing all who stood in their way. They went in search of the chief priests, who were soon captured and slain. The leadership of the aristocratic government was now over. Ananus b. Ananus was among the first to be executed along with his close associate Jesus b. Gamala, the man who had been responsible for trying to negotiate with the Idumaeans.

Then the nobility were arrested and thrown into prison and a series of trials were held. Josephus tells of the show trial of Zachariah b. Baruch, a rich aristocrat who was charged with treason, before a jury of 70 men. He was acquitted but the Zealots raised such an outcry that as he was preparing to leave two of them set upon him and slew him in the midst of the Temple exclaiming, 'Now you have our verdict also and a more certain release'.

However, this trial and execution appear to be the exception rather than the rule. There seem to have been few executions amongst the rest of the nobility, who remained imprisoned, and Josephus lists only a few names. Although he tells us that thousands died at this time, in reality the numbers were far fewer, perhaps only amounting to a few hundred.

With the collapse of the old regime the Zealots had to secure their rule. The countryside had rallied in defence of the capital, and a fresh upsurge of revolutionary fervour spread to the villages:

> In all the districts of Judaea there was an upsurge in terrorism dormant hitherto; and as in the body if the chief member is inflamed all the others are infected, so when strife and disorder broke out in the capital the scoundrels in the country could plunder with impunity, and each group after plundering their own village vanished into the wilderness.[8]

Josephus goes on to speak of these groups joining forces and organizing themselves into companies, smaller than an army but big bigger than armed gangs, so that every corner of Judaea was 'going the same way as the capital'. Josephus gives a more specific example when he speaks of events in eastern Idumaea on the shores of the Dead Sea. Here there stood a fortress, Masada, originally built by earlier kings. Herod the Great had expanded it to serve as a refuge in times of need against the two dangers he envisaged. First the Jewish people might rise up against him and depose him, second the fear of Cleopatra, Queen of Egypt, who had her sights set on regaining this part of the east for Egypt.

It took Herod a long time to build Masada, as the remains today testify, but eventually with the most detailed planning and aid of master craftsmen he succeeded in converting the desert cliff into a uniquely well-appointed fortress. Josephus describes Masada in the following manner. He [Herod] built a wall surrounding the mountain-top, seven stadia long; 12 cubits (5 m) high and 8 cubits (4 m) wide; and on the wall all round he built 37 towers. Herod also built himself a palace on the western decline, below the wall, which surrounded the peak, and everywhere Herod hewed cisterns out of the rock, and in that manner he was able to provide water for those living there as though there were springs at their disposal. Thus the fortress was fortified against any enemy who might wage war against it.

It was on this fortress a band of Zealots now made their camp. Josephus refers to them as *Sicarii* (dagger men). They had been here since the rebellion first broke out in AD 66 but according to Josephus they had merely raided the nearby districts to procure supplies, with the exception of one brief foray into Jerusalem. When they heard what was happening in the city, and that the Roman army was making no advance towards the capital, they immediately began to make more raids. The first was on Engeddi where they cut down its defences and took provisions which they brought back to Masada, this was followed by further raids in the area, all the time swelling their ranks with as Josephus calls them 'further ruffians like themselves from all sides'.

It is important to note the impression that Josephus gives may be a false one. It would not make sense for these 'bandits' to raid villages where they would naturally hope for support for the revolution rather than alienation. It would seem more feasible to suppose the raids and looting carried out was done to lands and property of the aristocrats.

Revolution raged in the countryside where thousands of Jewish peasants were still bearing arms against Rome, however Rome itself was also wracked with internal strife at this time (see the following chapter). Around Jerusalem many new strongholds of resistance were being created, from caves in the hills to the fortresses of Masada, Herodium and Machaerus, manned mainly by peasant farmers, who were now forming the heart and soul of the revolution. They relied upon the apocalyptic vision of the sects to provide the underlying ideology of the revolution, and also to provide the leadership needed to organize a diverse group of parochial peasants.

Power was now in hands of the radical militants, Eleazar the Zealot, John of Gischala and Simon the Idumaean. The Zealots had been in the Temple precincts longer than the others, however, they lacked numbers, according to Josephus only around 2,400 men in total. It is clear some of the Zealots were priests; one author has described them as 'militant traditionalists' and likens them to modern groups like Palestinian Hamas, or Lebanese Hezbullah.[9]

On the other hand John of Gischala led a greater force roughly 6,000 consisting not only of his Galilean followers but many new recruits who joined him when he arrived in Jerusalem, also to these numbers were added those existing militia men who allied themselves to him in a loose coalition. It seems that for a while John was the leading political figure in Jerusalem.

Josephus says John, in his words, out of a perverse desire for self-aggrandisement and power, broke away from the coalition. He was abandoned by a large number of antagonists who feared John sought monarchical rule for himself:

> Such then was the origins of the split in the party, and John confronted his adversaries as a rival sovereign. However their attitude to each other was purely defensive and there were seldom if ever any skirmishes in arms between them; but they were rival oppressors of the people and vied with each other in carrying off larger spoils.[10]

The other formidable army in the city were the Idumaeans. In the beginning they had taken their lead from the other groups for as already noted they had been called to the aid of the Zealots, which they had responded to, and then disbanded having no real political motivation to remain. However, some members did remain behind, according to Josephus in early AD 70 5,000 men were under the command of Jacob b. Sosas and Simon b. Cathas.

There was also a new revolutionary upsurge taking place in the villages of Idumaea and southern Judaea, led by Simon b. Giora. Eleazar was the leader of a millenarian sect who believed the final days were at hand, whereas Simon was the leader of a people's revolution whose aim was the emancipation of the peasants. Simon was a young, intelligent and charismatic figure, who Josephus says was held in 'special awe and respect' by his men.

Simon came from north-east Judaea the region of Acrabatene and joined the defence of Jerusalem earlier the war; in AD 66 he had commanded militia in the battle fought against the procurator Cestius Gallus. Despite this the government of Ananus placed little trust in him and he was given no government post but driven from Acrabatene and forced to seek exile in Idumaea. While in exile he formed an alliance with the Zealots at Masada but at the same time he had formed his own group of militia comprised of other Judaean exiles and Idumaeans.

With the overthrow of the government and death of Ananus, Simon saw his opportunity to make a challenge to John for the leadership of Jerusalem. He collected an army consisting in the most part of refugees from the Zealots camp, and when the Romans retired from the area in the middle of AD 68, he got control of the area of his previous command without opposition and held it against Zealot attack. He then invaded Idumaea. Despite putting up some resistance the district was finally handed over to Simon by a traitor, and many Idumaeans now joined his army. He created a fortified stronghold at a place called Nain where many new recruits joined him, including, according to Josephus, members of the elite.

Simon now proclaimed freedom for the slaves and rewards for the free. This is the message of the Jubilee, and presumably in those areas under his control slaves were freed and debts cancelled, as well as land redistributed. Josephus tells us he commanded armies between 20,000 and 40,000 strong and built many fortifications and storehouses, which implies this was turning into a peasant war.

In the spring of AD 69 Simon tuned his attention to Jerusalem and encamped outside the city walls. John and the Zealots had established themselves as leaders and had instigated a reign of terror. Both armies clashed outside the city but the Zealots were forced back by Simon and retreated into the city. The Zealots managed to capture Simon's wife but his treats of retribution if any harm came to her were taken so seriously she was returned unscathed.

However, Simon faced a more serious threat in Idumaea where conservative forces rallied to defend local properties. The first battle, which lasted a whole day, was inconclusive. Simon rallied a greater force and although he failed to take the Idumaean stronghold at Herodium, treachery and desertion from the Idumaean camp ensured the main Idumaean force was destroyed before a single blow had been struck. Josephus describes how such treachery came about:

> For this service James, one of their [Idumaean] officers, promptly volunteered, meditating treachery. He according set out from Alurus, the village where the Idumaean

army was concentrated, and repaired to Simon. With him he made a compact, first to deliver up his own native place, after receiving an assurance on oath that he should always hold some post of honour; he further undertook to assist in the subjugation of the whole of Idumaea.[11]

Simon was now in control of the south and the most powerful of all revolutionary leaders. There was only one place to go and that was Jerusalem, where the popularity of Eleazar and John was on the wane. This gave the conservative forces a chance to take over the leadership; the Idumaean militia in Jerusalem had broken with the radicals and formed an alliance with the High Priests, who had luckily mustered their forces. They had combined in an attack on the Zealots and Galileans and drove them from most parts of the city forcing them to seek refuge on Temple Mount and the royal palace on the Ophel hill to the south.

Simon had encamped outside the city, and was given access by the Idumaeans who had lost faith in the leadership of Eleazar and John. On gaining access Simon straight away began to oust the Zealots entrenched in the Temple. The split that had occurred between John and the Zealots a year earlier was further exacerbated, instead of them joining forces against the outside threat it became even deeper than before, and a three-cornered struggle began. The Roman historian Tacitus remarks: 'There were three different leaders and three armies ... until, on the approach of Romans, fighting the foreigner healed the breach between them'.[12] A small group of 2,400 Zealots under the leadership of Eleazar held the inner courts, while John's party numbering 6,000 held the outer court and part of the Lower City on the Ophel and fought on two fronts, between Eleazar and Simon. Simon had the greatest army numbering 15,000 and he controlled the Upper City and most of the Lower. As Simon held most of the Lower City, then presumably John held the rest as he did in AD 70.

One of the effects of the conflict was the burning of large stocks of grain, particularly serious if the year October AD 68–9 was sabbatical and fresh supplies were not available from outside. Before the next harvest gathered in April–May AD 70, Jerusalem was under siege and severe famine one of the hardships suffered; a consequence of which was the weakening of the rebel militia, unable through hunger to continue the struggle.

Simon's government had been brought to supreme power in March/April AD 69 and became as firmly established as John's had the previous year. It seems Simon managed to gain the support of many of the remaining ruling class including Ananus b. Bagadatus, who became responsible for overseeing the execution of deserters to Rome during the siege.

Simon's control of the city made the alliance between John and Eleazar no longer viable as far as Eleazar was concerned, and he hoped for an alliance with the more powerful group attached to Simon. It is not clear whether Simon accepted his alliance but John pre-empted any attempt at a new coalition by regaining the inner Temple by trickery and Eleazar and his supporters had to accept his leadership against Simon and Rome for the rest of the war.

The rebels were now confident of victory against the advancing might of Rome and the Jewish state functioned as if it were a permanent fixture. The best evidence for this comes from the rebel coinage issues of the period, 'which survive as testimony independent of Josephus' account of the war'.[13] Those of the fourth year (AD 69–70) are exceptionally well minted, and the coin types changed only slightly from the first issues, incorporating slogans that emphasized liberty and the holiness of Jerusalem. Even the Temple service continued up to the last days of the war, and although the inner court served as Zealot headquarters they allowed all those who wanted to enter to worship to do so. In fact it seems even pilgrims still flooded into the city right up to the time of its downfall, Josephus says:

> Of these [prisoners of Rome] the greater number were of Jewish blood although not natives of the place; for having assembled from every part of the country for the feast of unleavened bread, they found themselves suddenly enveloped in the war.[14]

Not even the campaign of terror tactics employed by the Romans throughout the rest of the country to demoralize and frighten the rebels seems to have been a deterrent to those in Jerusalem, who appeared to ignore the awful events that continued to take place in the rest of the country. It was obvious such terror tactics would be beneficial to the Romans, especially knowing Jerusalem's walls would be difficult to breach and any technique that could avoid the loss of thousands of soldiers would naturally be employed.

It has been pointed out:

> The Jews can be forgiven for being complacent, not understanding the complexities of Roman law or politics that rendered Vespasian's position simultaneously dangerous and advantageous after Nero's death, saw only the reluctance of the Romans to commit themselves to the fight.[15]

However, it is noted that Josephus offers another reason for Vespasian's hesitancy implying Vespasian's reluctance to advance on the capital was because he was waiting for civil dissension to destroy the rebels. This may well be a valid reason. Whatever the case, with hindsight, despite the confidence of the rebel forces their faction fighting was to prove to have been a costly mistake. Instead of using this time to unify a strategy, capitalizing on the fact the Roman campaign in Judaea was on hold, and preparing against the Roman advance, the rebels had been busy vying for supremacy of a new independent Jewish state, which was to be short-lived.

The chaos that ensued in Rome in AD 69 was reflected throughout the empire. Revolts occurred in north-east Anatolia led by Anicetus, the ex-commander of the royal fleet of Polemo II of Pontus whose territory had been taken over by Nero five years earlier, in Britain there was a rebellion led by Venutius in opposition to Queen Cartimandua and her Roman allies, and finally in Germany where Civilis sought independence from the Batavi tribe; Rome and its leadership were now on the brink of civil war.

11

Civil War in Rome

*The secret of empire was that now emperors could be
made in places other than Rome.* (Tacitus Histories 1.4)

The year AD 69 was also turbulent in the history of Rome, and the main reason
why the war in Judaea was put on hold. In early AD 68 the siege of Jerusalem
seemed imminent so Vespasian's decision to march the army out of Judaea
and back to the coast made little sense. Rebel territory had been reduced to the
desert area of which only a few strongholds remained, Macheraus, Masada and
Herodium, and these could have been dealt with quickly once Jerusalem had
fallen. The reason behind Vespasian's action was not a military decision but a
political one, for there was a major crisis occurring in Rome, where civil war had
been brewing for some time.

The crisis seems to have begun with the fall of the Senecan government in
AD 62. Seneca was a senior senator under the emperor Nero. He fell from power
that same year and was required to retire and relinquish his vast wealth to Nero.
In AD 65 he was forced to commit suicide after the failed plot by Piso. The collapse
of the government was followed by assumption of power, led by the emperor
Nero along with a small court faction, which consisted of the emperor's new
wife Poppaea Sabina and the praetorian prefect Tigellinus. Nero's extravagances
led to a crisis of confidence amongst the ruling classes who were concerned for
their safety and the safety of their property. It was also of major concern to them
that the empire was being bled dry to accommodate the emperor's proliferate
lifestyle which had already resulted in a series of rebellions throughout various
parts of the empire during the 60s AD, of which the Jewish one was by far the
more disturbing.

The Roman auxiliary troops on the Rhine had revolted and were joined
by Gallic chieftains and Druids. They managed for a short while to establish
an 'empire of the Gauls' in the western Rhineland and received massive local
support.

In AD 65, in a desperate attempt to remove the emperor, several members
of the aristocracy, including politicians, members of the army and intellectuals
including the poet Lucan, conspired to assassinate Nero and place Calpurnius
Piso on the throne. However, they were betrayed and a reign of terror was

instigated causing many to go in fear of their lives. This was no doubt initiated by Tigellinus, who Tacitus called Nero's evil genius. Informers were encouraged to denounce others and many people were no doubt wrongly accused by their enemies for conspiring against the emperor and forced to commit suicide. A situation not dissimilar to the 'Reign of Terror' during the reign of the emperor Tiberius, 30 years earlier and instigated by his 'evil genius', Aelius Sejanus, commander of the Praetorian Guard.

In AD 66/7 the emperor Nero made a fateful mistake when he executed the three most powerful generals of the empire, Rufus, Proclus and Corbulo. This further increased the fears of the aristocracy who felt if such action could be carried out on these men then they too would eventually fall victim to the emperor's whim. In AD 68 the end came in a rather unexpected way, when Helios the freedman who had been left in charge of Rome while the emperor was away, journeyed to Greece to persuade Nero to return. It appears Helios may have heard rumours of possible rebellion in Gaul, although the sources are not clear on this point.[1]

Consequently, Nero was persuaded to return. During the following year Julius Vindex, a Gallic nobleman and governor of Gallia Lugdunensis, led a rebellion in Gaul, inciting the population with his anti-Nero propaganda. In fact Vindex's uprising is remarkably similar to the revolt occurring in Judaea. Although Vindex wished for the liberty of Rome to be restored, more importantly his followers may have had a different motive being fired to rebellion by local discontent, rather than political matters in Rome.

Nero was slow to act. He had just appointed two new governors to control the Rhine legions, Verginius Rufus and Fonteius Capito; with the powerful Rhine legions in control then any threat from the Gallic tribes could be considered a minor threat. However, Vindex was in close contact with the governor of Hispania (Spain), Galba, and declared his support for him. Galba was an experienced general, appointed by the emperor Gaius (Caligula), and noted for his severity. However, he only had one legion under his command and needed more support other than that offered him by Vindex if he was to attempt to march on Rome.

Vindex forced his hand and proclaimed him emperor, so Galba declared his intention and soon received the support of other governors of the Spanish provinces, including Otho (the divorced husband of Poppaea Sabina, the new wife of Nero). Nero's position now began to disintegrate rapidly. Galba was a major political figure, and as such would have been able to rely on a large senatorial following as well as being able to secure the support of quite a few provincial governors. However, in terms of military strength Galba was weak as he only had one legion under his command, while Nero could call upon the mass forces of the empire.

Sometime later the governor of Africa, Claudius Macer, also made a bid for the throne, now Nero was threatened on two fronts, so he placed Petronius

Turpillianus in charge of the Italian forces. What happened next is not clear but Vindex apparently entered into negotiations with Verginius Rufus at the conclusion of which Rufus attacked and massacred Vindex's forces. Vindex took his own life, and when Galba heard the news he retired expecting his own death would soon follow.

In Rome Nero's position was collapsing; grain prices were rising; Turpillianus proved disloyal; the Roman political classes weighed up the possibilities and Nero found his support gradually disappearing. Sabinus, who had been appointed prefect of the praetorians decided, given all the available information, Nero would lose. Sabinus offered the soldiers a huge bribe if they switched their support to Galba, naturally they did and the senate legalized their position by declaring Nero a public enemy and declaring Galba emperor. The courtiers abandoned the imperial palace and Nero fled the city accompanied by only his closest associates. Accounts of his last days are full of fiction. Among many rumours circulating at the time were those that told of his plans to flee to the east, or retire to earn a living on the stage, something that may well have been true given Nero's fondness for music and drama. Sabinus persuaded the praetorians that by fleeing the city Nero had abandoned them and so they should move against the emperor. A contingent of cavalry was sent after Nero and in a suburb outside Rome Nero killed himself. Reportedly his last words were 'I such an artist, perish'.[2]

The death of Nero left Galba in a strong position, but this was to disintegrate in a remarkably short period, for Galba was unable to consolidate his support and more importantly severely overestimated his security. He killed many prominent men and his strict disciplinarian nature won him few friends. He embarked on a limited reorganization of the provincial commanders. The general Vitellius was sent to Germania Inferior and Flaccus to Germania Superior, while the east remained the same. He made no attempt to win over those who had supported Nero's regime and the troops raised by Nero remained in Rome; furthermore he did not attempt to reorganize the praetorians. A legion raised by Nero from members of the fleet petitioned Galba to remain legionaries but Galba refused so they became disorderly. Galba charged them with cavalry and brought them to order, then he proceeded to decimate them (a punishment that involved executing every tenth man). Galba also managed to lose the support of some of his former allies. For example, Otho received no reward for his loyalty and Caecina who had represented Galba at crucial moments in Germany also received nothing. Instead authority was placed in the hands of three members of the court, Vinius, who had led Galba's army, Laco a praetorian prefect and Icelus, a freedman.

By January AD 69 Galba's rule fell apart. It was customary for an oath of loyalty to be administered to the troops on the first day of the year. The German legions refused, mutinied and turned to Vitellius who was a popular leader. In Rome the praetorians also grew restless. Otho had ingratiated himself with officers and men by bribery. Galba responded by adopting Licianus a young nobleman as his heir, however the troops expected to receive a *donative* (a monetary payment) to celebrate the event. Galba refused and the troops became even more discontented.

On 15 January Otho staged a coup, which by all accounts appears to have been a rather disorganized affair. Galba's supporters tried to gather as many troops as possible but failed to find enough men. News began to circulate that Otho had been killed but as Galba and his supporters celebrated in the forum the praetorians arrived. Galba's supporters fled and Galba was ignominiously murdered.

> Near the basin of Curtius the panic of his bearers caused Galba to be flung sprawling from his chair. His last words are variously recorded by the conflicting voices of hatred and admiration. Some say that he grovelled and asked what he had done to deserve his fate, begging a few days grace to pay the bounty. The majority of historians believe that he voluntarily bared his throat to the assassins, telling them to strike and be done with it, if this is what seemed best for the country. Little did the murderers care what he said. The identity of the killer is in doubt. Some authorities speak of a veteran called Terrentius. Others mention one Laecanius. The more usual version holds that a soldier of the fifteenth legion named Camurius thrust his sword deep into Galba's throat. The rest of them with revolting butchery hacked at his legs and arms (as these unlike the rest of his body was not protected by armour). These sadistic monsters even inflicted a number of wounds on the already truncated torso.[3]

The accession of Otho did very little to appease the German legions so he had no other recourse than to prepare for conflict. First he needed to secure the loyalty of the troops in Rome and Italy and in this he was successful. He also managed to secure the support of the prominent generals. One of the reasons for his success was he associated himself with Nero even toying with the idea of calling himself Nero-Otho. He restored the statues of Poppaea and encouraged the exhibition of Nero's portraits. Nero's freedmen and procurators were restored to office and he continued building work on the Domus Aurea, the golden palace built by Nero after the great fire in AD 66 that had practically destroyed all the 14 quarters of Rome. Nero had been extremely popular amongst the plebeians, so much so many believed he was still alive and there were constant reports of sightings of him from all over the empire.

Otho also tried to win the support of his former enemies and those who had allied themselves to Galba. There were some exceptions but mainly all Galba's supporters were pardoned, including Celsus who had attempted to organize a military resistance against Otho; he was given a command. Potential enemies were also given some consideration, and with the appointment of Flavius Sabinus, the brother of Vespasian, to the important post of *Praefectus*

Urbi, this was accomplished. Rufus also achieved prominence being nominated for consulship. Those who had suffered under Nero and had their property confiscated, now had it restored, a very generous act given that the treasury was in a particularly bad state.

Otho also gathered sufficient troops in Italy to be able to resist Vitellius, and the approaching Danubian legions may well have tipped the balance in his favour had they arrived on time. On 1 January when the oath of loyalty was to be administered to the troops in Germania Inferior they had mutinied and refused to accept Galba as their emperor yet there was no declaration in favour of Vitellius instead they swore loyalty to the senate and the people of Rome. On 2 January Fabius Valens greeted Vitellius as emperor and by 3 January the legions of Germania Superior had also mutinied. It was at this moment that Vitellius began to organize his rebellion. The generals implemented an aggressive policy, Otho sent troops to Gallia Narbonensis where they had some success; however, the contest was to be decided in Italy. The military arm seems to have been led by Caecina and Valens they marched into Italy in two columns and achieved varying success, but at Bedriacum they managed to deliver the fatal blow against Otho, and consequently Vitellius was victorious. The defeat proved to be decisive but all did not appear to be completely lost. Surprisingly, rather than prolong the civil war, Otho on the advice of his friends chose to end it by committing suicide, after ruling for only 95 days. This is what the historian Suetonius has to say about his demise.

> the sensation caused by Otho's end was, I am inclined to think, largely due to its contrast with the life he had led. Soldiers who were present kissed the dead man's hands and feet, weeping bitterly and praising him as the bravest man they had ever known and the best emperor imaginable; and afterwards they committed suicide themselves close to his funeral pyre.[4]

The march to Rome from Germany had been slow and the Romans took every opportunity *en route* to extract money from the communities they passed through.

> On the outset of the march he had himself carried through the main cities of his route, in triumphal fashion; crossed rivers in elaborately decorated barges wreathed in garlands of many kinds; and always kept a lavish supply of delicacies available.[5]

The historian Dio Cassius also criticises the eating habits of Vitellius and the cost of his lavish meals. The march continued, then on reaching Italy there were clashes between the troops and the civilian population. The troops committed unspeakable acts of barbarity upon them:

> Not content with being feasted everywhere at public expense, they amused themselves by freeing slaves at random and then beating, whipping and wounding, and even murdering whoever tried to restrain them.[6]

Such was Vitellius' insensitivity that the numbers of dead civilians littering one nearby battlefield caused him to remark: 'Only one thing stinks worse than the corpse of an enemy and that is the corpse of a fellow citizen'.[7] Nevertheless he apparently took a good swig of wine to counteract the stink and then passed the flagon round.

Many of the aristocrats regarded the approach of Vitellius with some trepidation. While Otho had been successful in reconciling differences, Valens and Caecina had acted violently, and received no reprimand from their general, this brought doubts to their minds with regard to the attitude of Vitellius. With the death of Otho there was no suitable candidate to take his place so they were left with little choice. Sabinus administered an oath of loyalty to the troops in Rome and the armies of the eastern empire quickly followed suit.

Vitellius delayed accepting the titles of Caesar and Augustus although he did accept the constitutional powers that went with the titles. Vitellius appointed equestrians to the household offices breaking with the tradition of appointing freedmen. This was no doubt a tactic designed to try to reconcile the aristocracy to his rule.

He also tried to win the support of the Neronians by making funerary offerings to Nero in the Campus Martius in Rome. Vitellius staged lavish entertainments and even suggested Sporus, the ex lover of Nero, should appear on stage taking the role of a woman, however Sporus killed himself to avoid the shame.

The major problem for Vitellius was military. His troops had not inflicted a major military defeat on Otho, and the legions in the east were disaffected. Vitellius disbanded those praetorians that had shown loyalty to Otho and executed the Othonian centurions in the Danubian legions, which although may have removed potential enemies did little to endear him to the surviving members of the legions or their officers.

Vitellius' military insecurity meant he had to maintain a very large garrison, some 2,000 men in Rome alone, perhaps more to intimidate than to control and many of the men came from the legions in Germany. His problems were increased by the revolt of the Batavians led by Julius Civilis. This involved the auxiliaries Vitellius had recruited for his war effort, so he was unable to draw on reinforcements from these areas.

However the major threat was from the governors in the east. Initially the eastern armies (in Judaea, Syria and Egypt) had accepted Vitellius, but it seems this was only a temporary measure. On 1 July Julius Tiberius Alexander, prefect of Egypt administered the oath of loyalty to the troops stationed there in the name of Vespasian. By 3 July Judaea and Syria followed suit. The declaration had been a messy affair but the prompt action on the part of the Flavians (Vespasian and Titus) suggests it had been planned.

Mucianus the governor of Syria was sent west to lead the war effort while Vespasian went to Alexandria. The Danubian legions now took this opportunity to move against Vitellius and led by Antonius Primus they marched on Italy without awaiting the arrival of Mucianus. Although Vitellius had a large force in Rome and could call upon limited support from the western provinces, the Flavian forces were potentially overwhelming. As the legions crossed into Italy it seemed highly likely Vitellius would lose the war: this probably accounts for the defection to the Flavians of Caecina the leading general of Vitellius, however he was unable to bring his troops with him.

The two armies met at Cremona and fought a night battle which culminated in the rout of the Vitellian forces. The Flavian forces captured their camp and drove on to Cremona itself where the city was sacked. The Vitellians were defeated, though pockets of resistance continued. The Flavian troops began looting the city until the leader of the Danubian legions, Antonius Primus, eventually managed to drag them away to head for Rome. There were a series of minor engagements some of which produced limited successes for the Vitellian forces but the overwhelming numbers of the Flavian forces led to further defections from the Vitellian camp.

Vitellius entered into negotiations in Rome with Sabinus, Vespasian's brother. It seems he may have received assurances from Sabinus concerning his safety and so he abdicated, leaving the palace and entering the forum as a private citizen. As Sabinus organized the takeover the situation altered quite dramatically and Vitellius was retuned to the palace forcibly although there were demonstrations in his favour. The Flavian party seized the Capitoline Hill where they came under siege from Vitellian forces. During the siege the Temple of Jupiter Capitolinus, the most important temple in Rome, was destroyed, the Vitellian forces defeated the senators who were holding the Capitol, and Sabinus was executed. The younger son of Vespasian, the future emperor Domitian, managed to escape to safety.

> Domitian was concealed in the lodging of a temple attendant when the assailants broke into the citadel; then through the cleverness of a freedman he was dressed in a linen robe and was so able to join the crowd of devotees without being recognised and to escape to the house of Cornelius Primus, one of his fathers clients near the Velarum where he remained in concealment.[8]

The Flavian legions arrived on the outskirts of Rome but did not receive the expected surrender. Therefore they forced their way into the city, where the Vitellian forces fought a hopeless rearguard action across the city, resulting in the capture of the praetorian barracks. Vitellius fled the palace only to return later when he was captured and killed.

> Vitellius was forced at the point of the sword now to lift his face and offer it to his captors insults, now to see his own statues falling and to look again and again on the rostra or the place where Galba had been killed. Finally the soldiers drove him to the demonian stairs where the body of Flavius Sabinus had recently been lying. His only utterance marked his spirit as not ignoble, for when the tribune insulted him he replied 'yet I was your emperor' then he fell under a shower of blows; and the people attacked his body after he was dead with the same base spirit with which they had fawned on him while he was alive.[9]

Like his predecessor, Vitellius seems to have had notable political success. In the time from his appointment of command of the legions of Germania Inferior to his death in AD 69 he managed to win the loyalty of the German troops who had won two wars for him, many of whom lost their lives during the battles of Cremona and the last stand in Rome. He also won the loyalty of the people of Rome who supported him right up to the end. However, the major problem that led to his downfall was the fact he failed to resolve the tensions in the Roman state and win the loyalty of the Roman troops stationed there. In this respect like Otho and Galba before him he failed to win political legitimacy.

Vespasian, however, was in a far stronger position than Vitellius. He had the backing of the legions in the east and easily defeated the western legions, coupled with the fact the conflict in Germany and Gaul in AD 69–70 led to the defeat of the remaining forces in Germany. There was no substantial threat to challenge Vespasian, he numbered amongst his generals his eldest son Titus, Mucianus and some of Otho's generals who were also given positions of prominence.

When news reached Vespasian in the late spring of AD 68 of the death of Nero and the subsequent accession of Galba, Vespasian sent his son Titus, along with King Herod Agrippa to pay homage to the new emperor and obtain fresh orders for the campaign in Judaea. While they were on their way news reached them of Galba's untimely death, so Titus returned to Caesarea. Here, the generals met to discuss tactics and also to wait for the outcome of the impending conflict between Otho and Vitellius. When news finally arrived it was disastrous for the eastern legions. Vitellian forces now had control, which meant control of Rome was in the hands of the Rhineland forces. The historian Suetonius reports a rumour that Vitellius was intending to switch the western and eastern legions, forcing the later to exchange the relative comfort and ease of the city billets for wooden forts in the cold and wet German forests.

Josephus reports the mood of the troops prevalent in Vespasian's camp:

However his officers and men, in friendly gatherings were already frankly discussing a revolution. 'Those soldiers in Rome' they indignantly exclaimed 'now living in luxury, who cannot bear to hear even a rumour of war, are electing whom they chose to the sovereignty and in hope of lucre creating emperors; whilst we who have undergone numerous toils and are growing grey beneath our helmets, are giving up our privileges to others, when all the time we have among us one more worthy of the government. What juster return can we ever render him for his kindness to us if we fling away the present opportunity. Vespasian's claim to the empire is as far superior to that of Vitellius, as are we to the electors of that emperor; for surely we have waged wars no less arduous than the legions of Germany, nor are we inferior in arms to the troops we have thence brought back this tyrant.'[10]

Josephus implies that Vespasian was reluctant to accept the nomination and one can perhaps understand his hesitation, as the position was certainly a precarious one.

Their general had long been concerned for the public weal, but had never purposed his own promotion; for, though conscious that his career would justify such claim, he referred the security of private life to the perils of this illustrious station. But on declining, the officers pressed him more insistently, and the soldiers flocking with drawn swords, threatened him with death, if he refused to live with dignity. After forcibly representing to them his many reasons for rejecting imperial honours, finally, failing to convince them, he yielded to their call.[11]

However, it seemed an eastern coup was inevitable. Tiberius Alexander declared for him, which gave him both the Nile troops and of course the Egyptian grain supply. Later there were further declarations from Mucianus the governor of Syria and the Danubian legions whose revolt had been led by Antonius Primus. Vespasian now held the potential for success, he had the support of the whole of the east and the Balkans plus two of the three main army groups in the empire.

Vespasian then left for Antioch to deal with matters in Syria, instead of advancing west he moved his headquarters to Alexandria in Egypt and promptly cut off the grain supply to Rome. He then sent Mucianus with 20,000 men to Asia to gather further support. This was a precarious action to take and potentially damaging to the Flavian cause as it gave Vitellius time to regroup and re-militarize. However the actions of Primus thwarted this for he ignored any orders he may have received from Vespasian and crossed the Alps into the Po Valley determined to attack the enemy while they were still in disarray. For the second time in a few months the armies clashed at Cremona, and the Danubian legions were victorious.

With the downfall of Vitellius the senior officers installed a provincial government, headed by Vespasian's younger son Domitian. The empire now had a new emperor Vespasian, just as Josephus had prophesised. News of the Flavian victory in Rome did not reach Vespasian and Titus until the end of the year; Vespasian held court at Alexandria through the early months of AD 70 and then set sail for Rome. Before his departure he appointed Titus the new commander in Judaea with orders to capture Jerusalem and have the war finished by the summer. Titus was now in command of the largest army in the empire, and it was vital for the security of the Flavian dynasty he achieved a quick and resounding military victory. As one scholar remarks:

> The energy and disregard for the unnecessary loss of life among his own soldiers with which Titus prosecuted the siege of Jerusalem in AD 70 was entirely due to Vespasian's need to win a famous victory to justify his seizure of power, without that factor Roman hostilities against Judaea might have been as lackadaisical as those against Civilis on the Rhine.[12]

The battle for Jerusalem was now imminent and for the Jews their long-awaited apocalypse to herald the new age was about to begin with a vengeance.

12

The Battle for Jerusalem

Smite the nations, Thine adversaries, and devour the flesh of the sinner with Thy sword! (War Scroll DSS Qumran)

As a prior necessity to any attack upon Jerusalem, the areas that were held by the rebel leader Simon b. Giora had to be recovered and garrisoned by the Romans. These areas comprised north-east Judaea and Idumenaea. Once this had been achieved this left only the three fortresses of Herodium, Masada and Machaerus, plus a few pockets of resistance in the caves overlooking the Dead Sea, these were of little military consequence to Vespasian who chose to ignore them.

However, the Judaean campaigns had been halted early in July AD 69 when Vespasian was proclaimed emperor by his legions in the east and the Jewish war was put on hold. Vespasian and Titus went first to Beriut for a council of war, and it was here Josephus was finally released from his chains as a reward for the fulfilment of his prophecy, and became a useful ally to the emperor and his son. They then left for Egypt to secure the corn supply, so it was not until the spring of AD 70 action in Judaea was finally resumed; Vespasian transferred the Jewish command to his son Titus, while he returned to Rome to take up his now seemingly assured position of emperor.

In the early spring of that year Titus marched his army from the Nile Delta, along the north coast of Sinai and up the Levantine coast past Gaza, Ascalon, Jamnia and Joppa to arrive at Caesarea. He concentrated his main force here before beginning any further advances into Judaea. The Roman forces in Judaea now comprised four legions, the original V Macedonia, X Fretensis and XV Apollinaris and added to these numbers was the XII Fulminata from Syria, Titus also brought with him 2,000 men from the Egyptian legions, III Cyrenaica and XXII Deiotariana. The number of auxiliary units remained unchanged, but the client kings increased their contingents with Agrippa and Sohaemus personally leading their own troops. Tacitus tells us added to these numbers were:

Strong levies of Arabs, who felt for the Jews hatred, common between neighbours, and many individual adventurers from Rome and Italy, who for various reasons hoped to ingratiate themselves with the emperor whose ear might be gained.[1]

Tacitus also mentions 20 cohorts and eight *alae* and distinguishes between Agrippa and Sohaemus who contributed personally, and the forces of Antiochos and the Nabataeans, Agrippa had returned from Rome on hearing of Vespasian's proclamation as emperor. However, Josephus does not mention he was present at the fall of Jerusalem.

Tiberius Julius Alexander, the prefect of Egypt had been the first provincial governor to declare his allegiance for Vespasian and he now joined Titus' staff, which also included a new procurator of Judaea, M. Antonius Julianus. Josephus was amongst those who marched with the legions, now a free man and trusted by the emperor and his son. He was to act as a consultant on Jewish affairs, as well as translator and emissary. He describes the march of April AD 70:

> Titus advanced into enemy country behind an advance guard formed of the royal troops and all the allied contingents. Next came the pioneers [road makers] and camp builders, then the officers' baggage train: behind the troops protecting these came the commander-in-chief escorted by lancers and other picked troops and followed by legionary cavalry. These were succeeded by engines, and these by tribunes and prefects of the cohorts with a picked escort; after them and surrounding the eagle came the ensigns preceded by their trumpeters and behind them the solid column six abreast. The servants attached to each legion followed in a body, preceded by the baggage train. Last of all the mercenaries with a rear guard to keep watch on them.[2]

The two legions were encamped some miles behind, near the Jewish village of Gabath Saul. Because of the difficulty of maintaining supply lines in the Judaean hill country due to constant threat of guerrilla attacks Titus sent the other two legions in opposite directions, the V via Emmaeus and the X via Jericho. The following morning 23 April AD 70, a contingent of the Roman army appeared on the hills to the north of Jerusalem. It comprised a large body of cavalry over 500 strong sent out in advance to reconnoitre the area, and led by Titus himself.

The city of Jerusalem had been founded in the tenth century BC by King David, and had been a strong fortress from that time onwards. With its expansion over the centuries the city in the first century AD incorporated two spurs of land, on the eastern side was Temple Mount with the Ophel Hill immediately to the south. Overlooking Temple Mount was the Antonia fortress joining its north-west corner.

The western spur was much longer, wider and higher and terminated at Mount Zion. It was in this area the elite Upper City had developed during the Hasmonean and Herodian periods. At the north-western edge stood the royal palace, a strong fortress built by Herod the Great. In between the two spurs ran the Tyropoeon Valley. By comparison the Lower City was much older and accommodated the rest of the city's population. On three sides of the city there were deep ravines, the Hinmom Valley to the west and south and the Kidron Valley to the east between the Ophel Hill and Mount of Olives. The entire Upper and Lower City was enclosed by the 'First Wall' but on the southern side, where the city had continued its expansion, and incidentally where it was exposed to attack, the defences had been strengthened by two further walls.

The Second Wall went from the Antonia fortress in the east to the Gennath Gateway in the west. Its precise location is unknown but scholars believe it ran somewhere close to the royal palace. The Third Wall enclosed a larger area to the north where a new suburb known as the New City was under development on the Bezetha Hill. Herod Agrippa I had commissioned the building of the wall in AD 41–44 and massive stone blocks had been used in its construction, but because the Romans had become suspicious, Herod as client king and ally of Rome, had to abandon the project. The revolutionaries put the final touches to it and completed the wall. They raised its height to 9 metres (30 ft) at the level of the battlemented walkway, placing on it a series of square towers that projected from the wall at various intervals thereby giving a higher elevation.

This was the city that Titus viewed from the hills to the north. The city was surrounded by parched and infertile land, all the major trade routes bypassed it to the east, west and north. Its only real advantage was that the city was highly defensible. Titus assembled his army near Jerusalem, where one of the legions, the X Fretensis, established a base on the Mount of Olives, commanding the eastern side of the city while the other three encamped on Mt Scopus.

Titus rode down from Mt Scopus towards the main gate through the Third Wall. Before arriving at the gate he detoured to the right and made for the Psephinus Tower a tall octagonal building guarding the north-west corner of the Third Wall. His actions seem rather strange for he was approaching very close to the enemy with no military support. Not only that, the terrain was difficult for in many places it sloped steeply and was uneven. Also there were many ditches, walls and paths, surrounding gardens, orchards and olive trees. Not the most accessible of places, especially for cavalry who would be slowed down considerably as their horses tried to negotiate the rough terrain.

The approach of the Roman army now united the revolutionary factions in one common cause. The battleground was ideal for them, as in addition to the fortifications and difficult ground, the built up part of the city was a maze of narrow streets and alleys, and underground there were a series of water and sewer tunnels, which meant that sorties could emerge from any direction and take the Romans completely by surprise. The Jews organized themselves into small guerrilla units of about 200 to 500 men, and without the encumbrances of heavy armour they were able to move quickly and effectively unlike their armoured opponents. They were basically armed with javelins, slings and stones, but some were also equipped with swords, daggers and spears for close combat.

A small Jewish force made the first charge at Titus not long after he left the road and succeeded in cutting the Roman column in two. The Romans who had not yet left the road took flight leaving Titus and the rest cut off in the maze of orchards and gardens. Titus led a charge through a hail of missiles unleashed by the Jewish forces, and was very lucky to escape unscathed. Josephus tells us Titus had gone to reconnoitre and not to engage in a fight and had left himself vulnerable, as he wore neither helmet nor cuirass. The Jews: 'Thus successful at their first onset were elated with inconsiderate hopes and this transient turn of fortune afforded them high confidence as to the future'.[3]

The next day the rest of the army came to join Titus' force and work began immediately on the erection of three Roman camps, one for the XII and XV on Mt Scopus, three-quarters of a mile (1.2 km) to the north-east of the city, another camp for the V a short way behind this and the last camp housed the X on the Mount of Olives, about three quarters of a mile east of the city on the far side of the Kidron Valley. However, the Romans had not given enough thought to their plan, for the Jewish commanders from the city walls could observe them and get some idea of their strategy. Simon b. Giora had been responsible for the first attack as he and his militia controlled the Third Wall. Now with the Roman army building camps: 'The mutual dissension of the factions within the town, hitherto incessantly at strife, was checked by the war from without.'[4]

And the two rival factions united their forces for a large-scale sortie on the X legion encamped on the Mount of Olives. While the legion was busy encamping the Jews made a sudden and surprise attack. The Jewish force came out of the eastern and southern gateways of the city and swept across the Kidron Valley, storming up the opposite slope of the Mount of Olives and fell upon the Romans while they were still engaged building their fortifications.

> They [Romans] were therefore taken by surprise and thrown into disorder. Abandoning their work, some instantly retreated, while many rushing for their arms were struck down before they could round upon the foe. The Jews meanwhile were continually being re-enforced by others who were encouraged by the success of the first party, and with fortune favouring them seemed both to themselves and to the enemy far in excess of their actual numbers. Moreover men habituated to discipline and proficient in fighting in ordered ranks and by word of command, when suddenly confronted with disorderly warfare, are peculiarly liable to be thrown into confusion.[5]

The Romans made a stand but were overwhelmed by Jewish numbers and finally driven from their camp.

Titus immediately brought in reinforcements from Mt Scopus and rallied the legionaries. He then led a counter attack, which succeeded in driving the Jews back down the slope. The Jews retreated down the east side of the valley then made a stand on the western slope beneath the walls of the city. Here the Jews were safe, for the Romans would have had to pursue them uphill over broken ground risking attack by missiles from the walls above. There was now a stand-off until noon, when Titus thinned out the line facing the Jews across the valley and sent some of the legionaries back up the slope to resume work on the camp. Look-outs posted on the city wall signalled to fresh forces of Jewish fighters waiting at the gates and a second wave of Jewish fighters surged out to attack the weakened Romans. The Romans panicked and fled without even putting up a fight, so did the legionaries working on the camp the moment they saw the Jews crossing the valley and climbing up the slope.

Titus was isolated with only a few soldiers at his command and found himself in great danger. As Josephus notes this could have been the reason the officers on the ridge were now forced to rally the legionaries organizing a counter attack. The re-formed units now charged down the slope, and the Jews once again ran for safety on the far side of the valley. Titus now re-established his defensive line at full strength, so that the camp building could resume. From now on the Romans would be forced to post strong forces of cavalry and foot soldiers to prevent any further interruptions from Jewish sorties of this kind.

During the temporary lull in hostilities Josephus reports faction fighting once again broke out within the city. It was the Feast of Unleavened Bread and Eleazar gave orders to open the gates to admit those who wished to come and worship. John took advantage of this:

> Armed with concealed weapons the less conspicuous of his [John's] followers, most of whom were unspecified, and by his earnest endeavours got them stealthily passed into the temple to take possession of it. Once within they cast off their garments and were revealed as armed men.[6]

Wholesale panic ensued, as visitors to the Temple believed it was they who were being attacked and ran for shelter. The Zealots also not wishing to engage the intruders took refuge in the Temple vaults.

> Many peaceable citizens from enmity and personal spite were slain by their adversaries as partisans of the opposite faction, and any in the past who had offended one of the conspirators, being now recognised as a zealot was led off for punishment.[7]

John defeated Eleazar and they forced him into a truce, he had to accept John's leadership against the common enemies of Rome and Simon b. Giora; the three rival factions were now reduced to two.

For the Romans it was imperative the ground between their camps and the city was cleared of trees, hedges and fences, also ditches needed to be filled as well as rocks cleared to afford them a more level battle ground. This would also help render the guerrilla tactics less potent should the rebels decide to mount further sorties from the city.

However, the Jews were not so easily dismissed and they devised a further plan to catch the Romans off guard. A group of Jews came out from the towers along the northern side of the Third Wall and huddled together there as if in great fear of their lives. Others shouted from the battlements calling for peace and offering to open the gates, while at the same time pelting with stones those who were huddled by the wall. The ruse was designed to make the Romans believe the defenders had dispelled the majority of the war party from the city. A contingent of armed Jews was waiting behind the wall ready for the Romans should they fall for the trick.

Titus believed the peace party was in the majority and the previous day sent Josephus as his emissary to negotiate surrender. 'Josephus during his exhortation was derided by many from the ramparts, by many execrated, and by some assailed with missiles.'[8]

Josephus says Titus was suspicious of this action but many of his men were not and charged down to the gates expecting the Jews to surrender. They were received by a hail of missiles from the men in the front of the wall, and on the battlements; the party waiting behind the wall now surged forward and attacked them on both flanks. Fierce fighting ensued for some time until eventually the Romans managed to retreat back to their own lines. Titus was angry with his men for having broken the lines and rushing to the city without receiving orders to do so. Once again Titus had underestimated the ingenuity of the Jews.

The Roman army now completed the task of levelling the ground, but it was clear from the abortive negotiations and intelligence gathering that Jerusalem would be well defended and the task ahead would prove to be a difficult one. Titus was under orders from Vespasian to effect a quick and glorious victory to help establish the new Flavian dynasty in Rome, so a lengthy blockade was not really a viable option. It appears Titus chose the strategy of terror and treachery to achieve this end. Josephus was sent repeatedly by Titus to negotiate but was constantly met with a hail of abuse, his fellow Jews considered him little more than a traitor.

To approach the main defences of the city was a difficult task. First it was essential to mount an attack on both the Second and Third walls. The deep ravines of the Kidron and Himnom valleys made the possibility of a direct assault on the First Wall untenable. Only from the north where the ground was fairly even could any successful assault be contemplated. The Third Wall was also very strong along the majority of its length but there were places where it was weak, especially along the newly developed area of the New City. Titus' plan was to use ramps and battering rams to assail the wall.

Titus found such a weak spot in the wall somewhere near the Psephinus tower and the western gate, and redeployed his troops. He left the X encamped on the Mount of Olives and moved the other legions to two new camps about a quarter of a mile from the city, the V opposite the western gate, the XII and XV opposite the Psephinus tower. Once the baggage train had been successfully brought through by employing a line of men outside the north-western part of the city to prevent any Jewish skirmishes, work began on three earth and timber ramps.

The Romans erected wicker hurdles to protect themselves from missile attack and archers and artillery were also brought in to assist. Although there were a few sorties carried out by Simon b. Giora's men, the work progressed quickly. As soon as the distance between the wall and ramps was sufficient Titus ordered the advance. Artillery was moved closer to provide covering fire while the battering rams slowly moved up the ramps and into position, then he gave the order to strike. 'Suddenly from three different quarters a terrific din echoed round the city, a cry went up from the citizens within, and the rebels themselves were seized with a like alarm.'[9]

The rival factions united in their common cause and they joined forces on the battlements to rain down missiles on the Romans. Josephus gives a graphic description of the fighting that followed. Some of the braver Jewish fighters climbed on to the roofs of the rams tearing off the hurdles and pelting the soldiers with missiles. Firebrands were hurled from the battlements to set the engines alight and the Roman archers also came under fire.

> They hurled from them [the ramparts] firebrands at the machines and kept those who were impelling the battering engines under constant fire. The more venturesome dashed out in bands, tore up the hurdles, and falling upon the gunners, seldom through skill, but generally through intrepidity, got the better of them.[10]

During a lull in the fighting men from the western gate launched a surprise attack. This took the weary Roman troops off guard coming as it did from an unexpected direction. The Jews managed to get in among the engines equipped with firebrands. Some legionaries stood their ground while Titus counter attacked with his cavalry and drove the Jews back to the city before they had chance to do any serious damage to the engines. There were a few Jewish casualties and one man was captured; as an example to the others Titus had him crucified in front of the city walls. Also after the retreat John, the Idumaean leader, was killed by an Arab bowman as he was talking to an acquaintance in the ranks. His death came as a great blow to the Jewish forces.

The attack on the wall had lasted for about a week and by that time the Romans had mounted an iron plated wooden tower over 20 metres (65 ft) high on each of the three platforms, which made them too heavy to be overthrown by any Jewish sortie that might occur, of course it also rendered them virtually fireproof. The largest of the Roman rams was nicknamed *Victor* and on 7 May it finally punched a breech through the Third Wall forcing the defenders to take cover behind the Second Wall. This allowed the Romans to storm into the city and open the gates to the rest of the army. A section of the Third Wall was levelled and the Romans now occupied part of the New City, building a new camp in the north-western corner in the area known as the 'Camp of the Assyrians'.

The second assault began almost immediately and after four days one of the rams brought down the middle tower of the north wall creating a breech affording Titus the opportunity to deploy more than 1,000 legionaries into the suburb. There was a lull in proceedings and Titus' men were ordered not to plunder, while terms of surrender were once again offered to the rebels.

Titus then left behind a small garrison to hold the towers on the Second Wall and to defend the area beyond the breech. It appears many of the defenders had gone to ground and now they came from the gateways and infiltrated and surrounded the Roman position. As is usual in guerrilla warfare the Jews struck when the Romans dropped their guard. They assailed the Romans with missiles from the roofs and doorways with a constant stream of hit and run manoeuvres. The Romans formed tight blocks behind their shields and managed to make their way back to the breach, however they were now pinned down by the enemy. The garrison on the Second Wall also fled in confusion. The Jews moved up to the breach, only a narrow gap at the top of a heap of rubble, which allowed a few legionaries to pass through at a time, they also were assailed by a range of missiles from the Jews, it was only the arrival of a contingent of archers to provide covering fire that enabled the Romans to escape. The Jews then surged back on to the Second Wall and barricaded the breach, managing to hold it for three days against further Roman onslaught. However, on the fourth day the Romans broke back again and the Jews were forced to withdraw. This time Titus pulled down the whole of the northern section of the Second Wall and posted stronger garrisons in the remaining towers.

The fighting continued for almost two weeks; the battle for the Second Wall had proven to be particularly severe. Titus now suspended the siege for four days during which time he hoped the rebels would reflect on their situation and consider surrender. He also, as it was the legionaries' pay-day:

> Ordered his officers to parade the forces and count out the money to each man in full view of the enemy. So the troops as it was their custom, drew forth their arms from the cases in which 'til now that had been covered and advanced clad in mail, the cavalry leading their horses which were richly caparisoned. The area in front of the city gleamed far and wide with silver and gold, and nothing was more gratifying to the Romans, or more awe inspiring to the enemy, than that spectacle.[11]

Once again Josephus was sent to negotiate, he implored them to 'spare their country and their Temple and not to display toward them greater indifference that was shown by the foreigners'.[12]

Once again his pleas were met with a hail of missiles and the customary abuse. The Jews were now massed on the northern fortifications. John's militia with the Zealots held Temple Mount and the Antonia fortress at the eastern end. The Temple platform rose to a height of 45 metres (150 ft) above ground level and on top of this around the outer edge of the sanctuary ran a 12-metre (40-ft) high colonnade. Jewish defenders were deployed on the north and west colonnade. The Antonia fortress on the southern side was connected to the Temple colonnades by a series of access stairways.

Simon b. Giora's militia held the First Wall, which ran all the way through the city to the royal palace. There were three towers at the north-west corner, built of marble and rising to 40 metres high, surmounted by battlemented turrets and ramparts. The whole of the northern line stretched for 1,200 metres (4,000 ft) and was manned by 20 men for every metre; therefore the Jews had every reason to feel confident in their defence of the First Wall.

The key to taking the city was the Antonia fortress, and this was where Titus launched his campaign. He divided the four legions into two groups. The V and the XII to attack the fortress and the X and the XV to attack the First Wall. They began to build ramps, at the Antonia fortress they were positioned 10 metres (30 ft) apart and at the First Wall, 15 metres (50 ft). Immediately the Jews assailed them with a hail of missiles but despite their attempts to disrupt the work the ramps were finally completed on 29 May.

The Jews had no option but to wait for the attack. However, they had not been completely idle during this time, for John and his militia had been busily digging a mine from one of the tunnels that ran beneath the Temple platform. They excavated beneath the Antonia platform in order to run beneath the Roman platform. When the excavation was completed they would fire the props so to bring down the roof of the tunnel and consequently anything that was above it, hopefully the ramp. The Roman battering rams were already in place when the Jews fired the faggots coated in pitch and bitumen:

> The props being consumed, the mine collapsed in a heap, and with a tremendous crash the earthworks fell in. At first dense volumes of smoke arose with clouds of dust, the fire being smothered by the debris, but as the materials which crushed it were eaten away, a vivid flame now burst forth. The Romans were in consternation at this sudden catastrophe and dispirited by the enemy's ingenuity; moreover, coming at the moment when they imagined victory within their grasp.[13]

Three days later Simon launched a similar attack on the Roman ramps occupying the First Wall. Three fighters were sent out by Simon; they were Tephthaeus a Galilean, Megassarus a former royal servant and Ceagiras a disabled man from Adiabene.

> No bolder men than these three sallied out from the town throughout the war or inspired greater terror; for, as though racing for friendly ranks and not into a mass of enemies, they neither slackened or turned aside, but, plunging through the midst of the foe, set light to the machines. Assailed by shots and sword thrusts from every quarter, nothing could move them from the field of danger until the fire had caught hold of the engines.[14]

The attack was successful, and immediately both Jewish and Roman reinforcements rallied to the scene. The Jews won the day for the fires were soon raging out of control consuming the rams as well as the platform. The Jews now flushed with success rushed from the gates and attacked the Roman lines, eventually the Romans were forced to fall back through the narrow streets of the northern part of the city; gradually they were forced back to their camp. The guards on duty there were under strict orders to defend the camp otherwise they faced the death penalty. They held their ground with the aid of bolt shooters who had hastily been lifted on to the rampart, and managed to halt the Jewish onslaught. Titus arrived and improvised a counter attack on the right flank of the Jewish forces. The battle was a messy affair with the Jewish fighters being blinded by dust, finally they retreated behind the First Wall. It had taken the Jews only two days to destroy what had taken more than two weeks to build.

This incident had a demoralizing effect upon the Romans. They had already stripped the surrounding countryside of all available timber and even if fresh supplies could be brought in to make more platforms there was no guarantee the same situation would not arise again. Titus convened a council of war, where some argued for a full-scale assault by the entire army. Others argued for a starvation campaign to be levelled at the inhabitants of the city. Neither of these arguments was feasible for a variety of logistical reasons and it seemed the only recourse open to the Romans was to rebuild the platforms. It was paramount everything possible was done to limit Jewish activities, and this could only be achieved by privation and terror tactics.

13

The Final Conflict

Behold the beauty of what you are betraying; what a city!
What a Temple! What countless nations gifts! (JW 5:417)

Titus ordered a wall of circumvallation to be built around the whole of the city of Jerusalem. The wall was nearly 5 miles (8 km) in length and began and ended on the Bezetha Hill. Josephus says it was completed in only three days, and was strengthened by 13 forts, which were no doubt manned by the auxiliary troops.

This blockade took immediate effect on the population whose ranks had been swelled by large numbers of pilgrims arriving for the Feast of Unleavened Bread. It is estimated there may have been about a quarter of a million people in the city, all of whom had now to be fed. There were five possible sources of food supply available, the large warehouses on or beneath Temple Mount that housed the tithe and first fruit offerings; the stocks of grain the rebels had stockpiled before the siege began; private supplies of grain perhaps belonging to aristocrats or merchants; food smuggled into the city; and as Josephus says, any food that could be foraged from the immediate vicinity of the city. The Romans obviously had to limit the foraging and smuggling while at the same time put pressure on the use of those supplies held within the city.

There was not a completely tight seal around the city, many people, mainly aristocrats, were able to leave and seek refuge with the Romans. For their part the Romans saw them as potential allies for the future and welcomed them, however, lower-class people were not viewed in a similar vein and were subject to death or torture if they were caught fleeing. It is quite possible many thousands were crucified, a gory sight for those who watched from the walls of the city.

The defenders now faced famine; Josephus recounts a horrific story about a mother, who unable to find enough food, killed her own baby and roasted him, eating one half and offering the other half to a passing requisition squad. How reliable this story is we can only guess, nevertheless it is certain as the famine began to kill large numbers of people, such unspeakable acts were not uncommon.

At the beginning of the famine normal burial practices were enforced, paid for by the authorities but as the death toll mounted people became too weak to bury their dead. Bodies were dumped outside the city gates or flung from the walls, and here they remained for the rest of the siege, giving rise to infection and disease, which also took its toll on the population.

Famine and disease gave rise to fresh outbursts of dissension and there were numerous defections to the Roman camp. Simon, in an attempt to curb this exodus now unleashed a fresh wave of terror. The High Priest Matthias, who had incidentally originally welcomed Simon to the city, was arrested and charged with treason, along with his three sons. They were all executed and their bodies thrown over the wall.

> When Matthias entreated that he might be slain before his children, begging this favour in return for his having opened the gates to him Simon, ordered that he should be slain last. He was accordingly butchered over the bodies of his sons, who had been slaughtered before his eyes, after having been led out in view of the Romans ... Moreover he refused burial to the bodies.[1]

This was followed by the execution of two other members of the priestly class, Ananias and Aristeus, and 15 members of the aristocracy. However, there was further dissension amongst Simon's own men. An officer of his contingent guarding one of the towers with ten of his men attempted to defect to the Romans and were summarily executed. This action by Simon effectively stopped the threat of betrayal and mutiny and the peace party no longer became a threat to the revolutionary movement.

The Romans spent the following month working on the siege engines. No doubt Titus hoped the famine, disease, mutinies, crucifixions, and constant calls for surrender would wear down the opposition, especially as the Romans were well fed and continually taunted the starving population of Jerusalem with displays of food supplies. Knowing the tenacity of Jewish fighters Titus still had to make preparations for an assault, and concentrated all his efforts on the Antonia fortress. He sent his men as far as possible throughout Judaea to cut down trees until the whole area was a barren wasteland. With the new supply of timber they constructed four new platforms in 21 days. Josephus tells us about the mood that prevailed in both camps when the work had been completed.

> The completion of the earthworks proved, to the Romans no less than the Jews, a source of apprehension. For while the latter thought that, should they fail to burn these also, the city would be taken, the Romans feared that they would never take it, should these embankments too be destroyed. For there was a dearth of materials and the soldiers bodies were stinking beneath their toils and their minds under a succession of reverses. Indeed the calamities of the city caused more despondency to the Romans than to the citizens, for they found their opponents in no wise chastened by their severe misfortunes, while their own hopes were continually dashed, their earthworks mastered by the

enemies stratagems, their engines by the solidity of their walls their close combat by the daring of their antagonists. But worst of all was that the Jews possessed a fortitude of soul that could surmount faction, famine, war and such a host of calamities. They fancied the impetuosity of these men and their cheerfulness in distress invincible; for what would they not endure if favoured by fortune, who were impelled to valour by disasters? For these reasons then, the Romans strengthened yet more their guard upon the earthworks.[2]

In total the siege had been underway for ten weeks. The rebels had made a brave effort despite being in a weakened state. John and his party within the Antonia fortress, sallied out to attack the siege engines.

Having advanced with torches returned with ardent hopes grown cold ere they had approached the earthworks. For to begin with there seemed to be no unanimity in their design; they dashed out in small parties, at intervals, hesitatingly and in alarm, in short not like Jews.[3]

The Jews were defeated and made a retreat, the Romans now began to make an assault upon the wall using the battering rams with crowbars to lever out the stones at the base; the operation took all day and by the end of it all they had managed to accomplish was to dislodge four stones. All through the operation they were assailed by stones, firebrands and anything else the Jews could rain down on them from the walls above. It seemed like an impossible task but the weight on the engines plus the constant pounding caused the tunnel, originally excavated by John and his mining party in May, to collapse bringing down the whole of the northern wall of the Antonia.

Both sides were shocked by what happened. The Romans now faced yet another problem, for, anticipating the wall would fall, John and his men had built a roughly constructed second wall. In front of it was the heap of rubble from the collapsed first wall, and on either side the corner towers of the Antonia still commanded the approaches. It would be no easy task to storm the fortress, in fact little more than a suicide mission, so Titus called his best men and asked for volunteers.

Only 12 responded to Titus' request. A Syrian auxiliary called Sabinus led them and they launched a ferocious commando-style raid, which took the Jews by surprise. Although on their approach missiles hit several of his men, they succeeded in climbing the wall and scattering the defenders in front of them. However, it was a foolhardy venture, as they were few in number and had no back-up support; Sabinus tripped and fell, dying under a hail of missiles; of the remaining men three were battered to death by stones and their comrades carried the remainder, who had been wounded in front of the wall, back to the camp.

An alternative plan was to attempt a night-time assault Two days later in the early hours of 5 July, 20 infantry on guard duty manning the platforms plus a standard bearer, a trumpeter and two cavalry men, crept forward and climbed into the ruins of the Antonia. They found the Jewish sentries asleep, killed them and mounted the walls. The trumpeter sounded a signal summoning reinforcements, the shock of which caused the remaining Jewish sentries to flee for their lives.

Titus and his officers with a contingent of picked men rode into the ruins to consolidate the victory. The majority of the Jewish opposition had fled towards the Temple and the Romans now took the opportunity to follow them along the tunnels that had been used previously by John and his militia. John and Simon's militia joined forces and now made a stand to block the Roman advance; fighting ensued in the narrow tunnel entrances that lasted for several hours; the Romans were better equipped for close combat fighting being armoured unlike the majority of Jewish fighters. However, because of the narrowness of the tunnels the Roman were unable to call on support in order to mount a mass charge at the enemy. On the other hand the Jews had huge reserves of men backed up across the concourse and so were able to keep the Romans penned in at the entrances. At one point a centurion from Bithynia named Julian, who was apparently exceedingly strong, launched himself at the Jewish line scattering the men who stood in front of him. However, his hobnail boots caused him to slip on the pavement and he was immediately set upon:

> The Jews crowded round him on all sides and struck at him with spears and swords. Many a weapon he parried with his buckler, many a time he tried to rise but was thrown back by the number of his assailants, and prostrate though he was, many a one did he stab with his sword; for being protected in every vital part by helmet and cuirass and drawing in his neck, he was not quickly despatched. At length when all his limbs were hacked and no comrade ventured to his aid he succumbed.[4]

It would appear the Romans' planned attempt on Temple Mount was doomed to failure and consequently the Roman contingent was ordered to pull back. There was a lull in the proceedings; then Titus ordered the walls of the Antonia to be demolished to create a breach through which the Roman army could storm Temple Mount. Josephus was sent once again to appeal to the Jews to surrender and encourage them to abandon the rebel cause.

> Josephus standing so that his words might reach the ears not only of John but also of the multitude delivered Caesar's message in Hebrew with earnest appeals to them to 'spare their country, to disperse the flames that were already licking the sanctuary and to restore to God the expiatory sacrifices'. His words were received by the people in dejection and

silence; but the tyrant after many invectives and imprecations upon Josephus ended by saying that he could 'never fear capture, since the city was God's'.[5]

It would be feasible to suggest that the speech was delivered in Aramaic rather than Hebrew.

On 17 July the Romans prepared for a final assault on the Temple. The priests had been forced to suspend the daily sacrifice because supplies of lamb had run out, and this was seen by many Jews as an omen of impending disaster.[6] Quite a number of the High Priestly families had deserted to the Romans, as well as many aristocrats, it seemed only the militia men remained unswerving to the cause.

Titus employed different tactics for this assault. He took 30 of his best men from each century and employed them in the line, grouping the men in 1,000-strong cohorts, commanded by tribunes. Sextus Cerealis commander of the V legion led the attack. Titus and other senior officers watched from an observation post situated in one of the towers on the Antonia. During the early hours of the morning the legionaries, comprising in all roughly 7,000 men, advanced slowly hoping to find the Jewish sentries asleep. The sentries, however, were not asleep and raised the alarm, bringing the militiamen out to form defensive lines. The front ranks came to halt and the army concertinaed on itself, the ranks behind stumbling in the darkness. The result was, in confusion, Roman turned upon Roman. However, the same thing happened on the Jewish side whose line was also in a shambles, being badly organized the men collided into each other in the darkness. When it became light:

Parting into their respective lines, they could employ their missiles and maintain their defence in good order. Neither did either side give way or relax their efforts. The Romans as under the eye of Caesar, vied man with man and company with company, each believing that the day would lead to his promotion, if he but fought with gallantry. The Jews had an arbiter of their own daring deeds their fear for themselves and their Temple and the looming presence of the tyrant, encouraging some, rousing others by the lash and by menaces into action, the contest was perforce for the most part stationary the manoeuvres to and fro; being limited to a narrow space and quickly over; for neither side had room for fight or pursuit. And at every incident of the fight an appropriate roar went up from Antonia; were their comrades gaining they shouted back to them to be of good cheer, were they falling back, to stand fast. It was like a battle on the stage, for nothing throughout the engagement escaped the eyes of Titus or of those around him. At length after an action which had opened at the ninth hour of the night, they broke off at the fifth hour of the day, neither side having seriously repelled their adversaries from the very spot on which the conflict began, and victory remaining undecided in this drawn battle.[7]

The Romans were unable to break through probably because the front was too narrow not allowing a strong enough force to engage the enemy at one attempt. We must also assume the Romans came under missile attack from the colonnade rooftops. Failing to effect a breakthrough they found themselves in a tactical impasse, and so at noon the commander called off the attack.

The Romans were massed near the ruins of the Antonia, the Jews on the northern side of the inner court of the Temple. The Jewish resistance was relentless; there was a raid to capture Roman horses left to graze by cavalrymen and a large-scale attack on Roman outposts on the Mount of Olives. The rebels also set about strengthening their defences on Temple Mount destroying a large section of the northern and western colonnades where they joined with the ruins of the Antonia making a gap of about 10 metres (30 ft) between theirs and the Roman positions.

On 27 July they also managed to set a successful trap for the Romans who were at work on a platform against the western colonnade. The northern extent of the colonnade had been almost completely destroyed by the Romans and they were now busy raising a platform near the broken end. The Jews secretly filled the space between the rafters and the ceiling with dry wood, bitumen and pitch, a highly flammable combination. They then feigned a show of leaving this section of the colonnade; the Romans saw an opportunity to mount an assault and ran forward with ladders. Hundreds of them reached the top of the undefended wall and climbed on to the roof of the colonnade, whereupon the Jews ignited their fire trap and engulfed them in the flames.

> The flames suddenly shooting up on every side, those of the Romans who were out of danger were seized with dire consternation, while those involved in it were utterly helpless. Surrounded by the flames, some precipitated themselves into the city behind them, some into the enemy's midst; many in the hope of saving themselves leapt down among their friends and fractured their limbs; but most in their rush to escape were caught by the fire.[8]

The whole colonnade from the north-west corner as far as the western gate was destroyed. Titus now ordered a fresh assault on Temple Mount. It was early August, the height of summer, and for several days the battering rams pounded at the walls using a specially constructed giant ram while working parties attempted to lever stones from the base of the walls with crowbars. The rams made no impression on the massive blocks of stone; the men working on the base had little success either. The breaching of the walls was abandoned and Titus ordered them to attempt to scale the walls instead; an action that would result in heavy casualties for the Romans, so an obvious act of desperation on their part.

As the men began to scale the walls their ladders were pushed away by the defenders. The Romans employed covering fire from missile shooters to keep most of the defenders away from the battlements, so the Jews waited until the legionaries came on to the walkways and then assaulted them, some were pushed backwards onto their comrades beneath; others were killed before they had time to cover themselves with their shields. The assault was once again proving a failure so Titus finally abandoned the attempt and ordered the gates and colonnades to be fired.

For the next 24 hours the Romans worked at destroying the gates and colonnades by fire, burning out the complete length of the northern colonnade right up to the north-east corner of Temple Mount. They then extinguished the fires so the engineers could clear the debris and make a smooth pathway for further assaults.

The Jewish position was now untenable, without the colonnades they could only man the walkways with a single line of men who had no access for a retreat as there was a sharp drop behind them, so they were forced to re-form their line across the middle of the sanctuary. The left side was anchored on the western gate linked with the Upper City by a bridge that spanned the Tyropoeon Valley and defended by a tower. The right rested on the eastern colonnade of the sanctuary, while the centre ran through the Temple and Inner Court.

A large balustrade ran around the outside of the Inner Court and inside this was a high, stepped, rectangular podium surrounded by a massive stone wall. There were four gateways on the northern and southern sides and an even more splendid one on the eastern side aligned to the entrance of the Temple. Colonnades and chambers ran round the inside of the wall providing a wide roof for fighting platforms about 20 metres (65 ft) higher than the surrounding sanctuary concourse. The eastern section formed the Court of Women, the western section was elevated above this on a second podium and beyond the Corinthian gate which passed through the middle of the wall was the Court of Israelites and beyond this the Court of Priests. Beyond the altar raised on a third platform was the Temple. It stood about 45 metres (150 ft) with a white marble and gold front façade. There was a covered entrance porch, which gave access to a pair of enormous golden gates and beyond these concealed behind the curtains was a Holy place where sacred objects were stored; at the furthest recess of the complex, the Holy of Holies, a sparse undecorated room entered only once a year by the High Priest.

The Jews now fell back against the advancing Roman forces, and took up positions on the rooftops of the Inner Court and Temple. Amazingly they were still able to manage to mount sorties despite their weakened state, and on 9 August they sallied forth from the eastern gate. The Romans were surprised by the attack but managed to hold their ground while Titus deployed a cavalry counter attack into the Jewish mass. The battle raged for three hours until the Jews unable to make any impression on the Roman lines retreated to the Inner Court. The following day the Jews attacked the legionaries holding the Outer Court but an incident brought disaster upon the rebels and initiated the beginning of the end. A soldier managed to hurl a firebrand through the window of one of the chambers of the Inner Court. The place immediately caught light and was soon full of thick black smoke and flames. There was chaos as the rebels desperately tried to save their holy place while at the same time beat off the Roman advance. The Roman lines now surged forward and managed to break through into the Temple.

Josephus' account of the incident may be a little suspect given he was the official biographer of the Flavian emperors. He says that Titus argued against an attack on the Temple but he also says he was present in the thick of the fight. However, there is other evidence probably deriving from Tacitus that Titus argued for the utter destruction of the Temple so to wipe out the religion of the Jews and Christians once and for all.[9]

It has been suggested that the ambiguity in Josephus is suggestive of the historian's attempt to understand the contradictory actions of the Flavians, who on the one hand seem intent to abolish permanently the cult of the Temple, while on the other upheld the Jews' right to observe their ancestral law. Any slight hesitancy on Titus' part may have be seen by Josephus that the Flavians were not actually hostile to Jewish tradition.[10]

As more fires began to rage the Romans ploughed on massacring all who stood in their way. John and Eleazar's militia managed to fight their way through to the southern gateways and fled across the Outer Court. Inside the Temple those left used any means they could to defend themselves. Priests even tore down the golden spikes that kept the birds off the roof and hurled them at the Romans, while others with all hope lost threw themselves into the raging fires.

> While the Temple blazed the victors plundered everything that fell in their way and slaughtered wholesale all who were caught. No pity was shown for age, no reverence for rank; children and greybeards, laity and priests alike were massacred; every class was pursued and encompassed in the grasp of war, whether suppliants for mercy or offering resistance.[11]

The siege was now transformed into total annihilation. The population of Jerusalem was trapped within an area that covered roughly 1 square mile (2.6 square km). For nearly a month the Jews found themselves at the mercy of the Romans. There were no rules, no code of conduct, what followed can only be described as horrific with barbaric acts performed on militia and civilians alike, no one young or old escaped Roman wrath and vengeance.

As for the Jews they had no recourse other than to believe God would deliver them from this carnage. A would-be prophet told the people such a thing would happen if they were to assemble at the Temple. A crowd of men, women and children all unarmed massed on the roof of one of the outer colonnades. They were spotted by the legionaries, who then set fire to the colonnade below. In desperation some flung themselves to their death, others perished in the fire; not one remained alive.

The Romans now set about plundering the Temple of its treasures. The Temple was not only a religious place, but had also acted as a repository for the wealthy who placed their money and valuables here for safekeeping as well as housing the money given in offerings and of course the Temple tax. It also stored tithes and other valuables dedicated to the Temple by vows of valuations.[12]

Titus had been in the thick of the battle and was cheered as the Roman standards were brought forward. An ox, sheep and pig were sacrificed before the eastern gate in contravention to Jewish religious susceptibilities while the legionaries chanted 'Imperator, Imperator' in honour of their leader.

However, there was still a small pocket of resistance; Simon's militia remained firmly entrenched in the Upper City and John's men, those who managed to escape the fall of Temple Mount, joined them there. There were still many thousands of rebel fighters left and they held some strong positions including the royal palace, which occupied the highest peak. It was advantageous to both sides to parley and they met on the viaduct, the bridge that spanned the Tyropoeon Valley between the western gate of the sanctuary and the gymnasium on the eastern slope of the Upper City.

Simon and John sought permission to pass through the Roman cordon with their women and children and go into the wilderness. However, Titus would not agree to this and offered them a choice between slavery or execution. In fairness to Titus he had no other recourse, because to release them meant reinforcing the opposition in the south, he had the main enemy force at his mercy and he needed to secure the capitulation of Jerusalem and destroy the revolutionary movement once and for all.

> Thereupon Titus indignant that men in the position of captives should proffer proposals to him as victors, ordered proclamation to be made them neither to desert nor to hope for terms any longer, for he would spare none; but to fight with all their might and save themselves as best they could, because all his actions henceforth would be governed by the laws of war.[13]

The following day the war resumed. The Romans fired the greater part of the Lower City clearing it of rebels within two days. Simon and John now turned the royal palace into a citadel for those rebels who remained. They ordered the public execution of two Roman prisoners, the first was killed and dragged around the city; the second was about to be beheaded when he managed to escape back to the Roman lines, where he was dismissed for having allowed himself to be taken prisoner in the first place. Simon also had five Idumaean leaders arrested and executed because they had been attempting to negotiate secretly with Titus. The rebel leaders were sending a message to the Romans that there would be surrender; this was to be a war to the death.

Once again the Romans were forced to begin building new platforms because the royal palace was impossible to scale. On 20 August the four legions were set to work in the Hinnom Valley and spent the next two and a half weeks constructing the platforms against the western palace wall. At the same time auxiliary troops were constructing platforms near the viaduct, gymnasium and Simon's tower. The work was slowed down by missile attacks from the Jews but they were slowly getting weaker as the famine continued to take its toll, therefore the attacks became less effective. Many now deserted the rebel ranks. A group of aristocrats surrendered and were detained, later they would be sent to Rome as hostages. Those citizens who defected were judged by a military assize and freed if they were found to be 'respectable'. Presumably this meant those wealthy enough to purchase a free passage.

We are told about some who managed to bribe their way to freedom, including a former Temple treasurer, a priest called Jesus who negotiated his safe passage by smuggling out a hoard of Temple treasure. However, the majority who defected were not in a position to offer any such inducements and consequently they were enslaved.

Several interesting points have been made when considering the role of the aristocracy in the rebellion. Despite what Josephus has to say about the war being mainly the work of the rebel militias there is ample evidence to show the ruling class remained loyal to their cause, right up to the closing stages of the war. The 2,000 members of the ruling class who had been released from prison by the Idumaeans in AD 69, apparently chose to remain and support the 'free Jewish state'. There were no physical restraints to stop them leaving at any point during the siege. In fact Josephus' brother and 50 of his friends were captured in the fall of Jerusalem, all presumably members of the elite and all actively participating in the fight against the Romans.[14]

On 7 September the platforms built against the royal palace were completed and the rams brought into position. Some of the rebels abandoned the wall, and those who remained fired at the Romans, however this was quickly suppressed. Soon the rams brought down sections of the wall, and legionaries stormed through the breaches virtually unhindered. The rebel leaders had taken refuge in the three northern towers but they too were now abandoned without a fight. They fled attempting to find a way round the Roman cordon, some even hid in the sewers. The revolutionary army was now a disintegrating mass of frightened stampeding men. The revolution was over and the inevitable sack of the city about to begin.

The Romans now masters of the wall planted their standards on the towers, and with clapping of hands and jubilation raised a paean in honour of their victory. They had found the end of the war a much lighter task than the beginning; indeed they could hardly believe that they had surmounted the last wall without bloodshed, and, seeing none to oppose them were truly perplexed.[15]

Josephus then gives a graphic account of what followed.

Pouring into the alleys sword in hand they massacred indiscriminately all whom they met and burnt the houses with all those who had taken refuge within … running everyone through who fell in their way, they choked the alleys with corpses and deluged the whole city in blood.

The city had finally fallen to Roman forces. Titus ordered the walls of the city to be levelled, except for Hippicus, Phaesal and Mariamme towers and a stretch on the western side, which was retained as a fortification for the Roman garrison. The V, XII and XV legions returned to other stations in the east, while the X legion with some auxiliaries remained behind to man the garrisons. Recent excavations have revealed that the X legion was stationed in Jerusalem until the first half of the third century AD.[16]

The *Pax Romana* (Roman Peace) was now instigated and the terms were harsh. First the Temple was not to be rebuilt, second the High Priesthood and the Sanhedrin were to be abolished, finally the Temple tax was to be paid directly to Capitoline Jupiter, which of course meant it went straight to the Roman treasury. Worst of all most Jewish lands now became Roman property and therefore the peasants would be tenants of the emperor. These measures were flames to fan the fighting spirit of those insurgents who still remained at large in the southern Judaean desert. Jerusalem may have fallen but the Jewish war with Rome was not yet completely over.

14

The Zealots' Last Stand

*Long ago we resolved to serve neither the Romans nor
anyone else but only God.* (JW 7:386)

Before leaving Jerusalem for Caesarea Titus organized a victory celebration in
the Roman camp. He delivered a speech to his men, and rewarded those who had
been valiant by crowning them with golden wreaths, promoting each individual
to a higher rank. The legionaries also held their own victory feast where huge
numbers of bullocks were sacrificed, and they also were rewarded with booty for
the spoils were indeed vast; nevertheless the majority of the treasure was reserved
for the triumph in Rome.

Josephus too received payment:

> Again, when Jerusalem was on the point of being carried by assault, Titus Caesar
> repeatedly urged me to take whatever I would from the wreck of my country stating, that
> I had his permission. And I, now that my native place had fallen, having nothing more
> precious to take and preserve as a solace for my personal misfortunes, made request to
> Titus for the freedom of some of my countrymen; I also received by his gracious favour
> a gift of sacred books. Not long after I made my petition for my brother and fifty friends,
> and my request was granted.[1]

The vanquished Jews were paraded in a splendid triumph in Rome; an event
Josephus witnessed. John of Gischala and Simon b. Giora the rebel leaders, were
in chains as the procession made its way through the city heading for the Sacred
Way. Tableaux and models were presented on immense moving stages, three or
four storeys high depicting scenes from the war.

> The war was shown by numerous representations, in separate sections affording a vivid
> picture of its episodes here was to be seen a prosperous country devastated, there whole
> battalions of the enemy slaughtered; here a party in flight, there others led into captivity;
> walls of surpassing compass demolished by engines, strong fortresses overpowered,
> cities with well manned defences completely mastered and an army pouring within
> the ramparts, an area all deluged with blood, the hands of those incapable of resistance
> raised in supplication, temples set on fire, houses pulled down over their owners heads

and after a general desolation and woe, rivers flowing not over a cultivated land but a country still on every side in flames.[2]

The Holy treasures taken from the Temple, including other precious ornaments, were also displayed. The procession contained 700 Jewish fighters selected for their size and physique, dressed in elaborate garments. They had been selected six months earlier from those who survived the manhunts after the fall of Jerusalem. Some prisoners had been killed immediately; those who were found guilty of terrorism were executed; while those who would be fit to grace the triumph were imprisoned. The rest who were 17 years of age or over were divided into two groups, some being sent to the imperial mines and quarries in Egypt, the rest destined for the arena.

The Jewish leaders John and Simon were also displayed in the triumph; there is no record of what happened to Eleazar. John had hidden underground at the closing stage of the war; he had given himself up when his food supply ran out. Simon on the other hand had remained active, trying to make his escape. He and a small band tried to dig their way out but the distance was too great and when their supplies ran out Simon tried a ruse. He dressed up in a short white tunic and crimson cape and appeared among the ruins of the Temple, presumably to frighten the Romans; although Josephus does not elaborate upon what Simon's exact intention was. The Romans were shocked but not panicked by his actions; he was arrested, put in chains and sent to Titus who by now was in Caesarea.

While John was condemned to life imprisonment Simon faced a worse fate. When the triumph arrived at the temple of Jupiter on the Capitoline, Simon was pulled to the ground and dragged across the forum. As he passed through he was scourged, a particularly unpleasant torture as the metal scourges ripped strips of flesh from the victim's body. Then at the place reserved for public executions he was executed by slow strangulation. The death of this most charismatic of all the freedom fighters was greeted by a resounding cheer from the crowds, followed by a great feast.

> After the announcement that Simon was no more and the shouts of universal applause which greeted it, the princes began the sacrifices, which having been daily offered with customary prayers, they withdrew to the palace. Some they entertained with a feast at their own table; for all the rest provision had already been made for banquets in their several homes. For the city of Rome kept festival that day for her victory in the campaign against her enemies.[3]

Some modern scholars are disturbed by what appears to be any lack of emotion on Josephus' part to the display of the Temple treasures and the victory of the

Romans over his fellow countrymen. Why does he not lament what has happened to his country? Instead Josephus describes at some length the triumph and the objects taken from the Temple in a very matter of fact way. After describing the rest of the triumph and festivities he then jumps ahead to the completion of the Temple of Peace built in AD 75 by the emperor. He says that Vespasian displayed items that had been the focus of attention for tourists from all over the world before this collection was on view. He specifically mentions the Law and the purple hangings were kept at the palace. Josephus' emphasis on upon the Temple objects and their new home reflects the attention drawn to the Temple throughout the whole text. We might well question whether 'Josephus is setting up for his readers a mental comparison between the relative grandeur of the Jewish Temple and the monuments of Rome'.[4] It is possible Josephus arranged his text for a reason, to provide that very vivid view of the Temple, even after it had been destroyed. In fact one scholar believes Josephus was making an active political statement. Whether or not his readers in Rome chose to believe or act upon it was another matter.

In the years that followed the fall of Jerusalem there were still pockets of rural insurgency in southern Palestine. The region was mainly a wasteland and Roman campaigns in AD 68/9 had largely been limited and indecisive. Many groups of revolutionaries were still operating here with typical guerrilla tactics, not wishing to be caught in cities that were under siege.

After the fall of the Holy city in AD 70 many fighters had managed to escape and made their way south to join these various groups. Josephus says they managed to form at least one new major base of operations at a place called the Forest of Jardes; its exact location is unknown. There also still remained in rebel hands the three desert fortresses of Herodium, Machaerus and Masada. The Romans adopted a systematic approach to the capture of these rebel strongholds by working their way out from Jerusalem and dealing with the stronghold nearest the city first.

Herodium was about 10 miles (16 km) south of Jerusalem on the edge of the Judaean desert and was the first to fall. This was another fortress built by Herod, its appearance was of a steep-sided cone containing on the top the palace fortress, which is where the rebels had entrenched themselves. The only access was by an underground passageway that led up from the bottom of the hill; a high casement wall and four projecting towers protected the summit, and there were abundant store-rooms and cisterns in the thickness of the cone, built specifically to withstand a siege.

The emperor ordered the destruction of these strongholds and left the task to Lucilius Bassus who had been despatched to Judaea as governor of Palestine. He had served Vespasian during the civil war, and for the first 18 months of

Vespasian's reign had been equestrian prefect of the fleets at Misenum and Ravenna; with him came the first post-war procurator Laberius Maximus. In the case of Herodium, Bassus seems to have succeeded without a great deal of difficulty, for the defenders quickly surrendered, we have no clue why they did so, or what terms were offered.

Bassus then led the army across the Jordan into south Peraea to attack the second fortress at Machaerus, which lay a few miles east of the Dead Sea. This fortress had been built by the Hasmonean kings during their conflict against the Nabatean Arabs and was later rebuilt as another palace fortress by Herod. It was a flat-topped rocky eminence surrounded by barren uplands, but was well protected by ravines and steep slopes, strengthened with walls and towers around the summit.

Bassus ordered a ramp to be built along the western approach to the fortress, and the Jews countered with the usual regular daily sorties. However, some of the Jews became reckless and one young fighter called Eleazar was captured. Bassus threatened to have him crucified in full view of the whole city, and began by having him stripped and scourged.

> At which sight those in the fortress were seized with deeper dismay and with piercing shrieks exclaimed that the tragedy was intolerable. At this juncture moreover, Eleazar besought them not to leave him to undergo the most pitiable of all deaths, but to consult their own safety by yielding to the might and fortune of the Romans, now that all others had been subdued.[5]

At this point the resistance of the defenders collapsed, and the city surrendered in order to save him. The people had asked for clemency, and were promised it, however when the Romans arrived all the men numbering 1,700 were slain and the women and children taken into slavery. By way of compensation, however those who had actually offered surrender Bassus let depart unharmed and to Eleazar he gave his freedom.

The Romans then marched on towards the Forest of Jardes where many of the refugees from Machaerus and Jerusalem had collected including a militia commander who had made his way through the Jerusalem sewers and had slipped unnoticed through the Roman lines. Bassus threw a cavalry cordon round the forest to prevent anyone escaping, then sent in the infantry to cut down the trees. The Jews attempted to break out by launching a series of attacks on the Roman lines, but each one was repulsed and the Jews driven back. After a lengthy fight the entire force was wiped out with the loss of only 12 Roman legionaries.

Also at this time the emperor sent instructions to Bassus to bring all Jewish territory under imperial control in accordance with the terms of the *Pax Romana*. He also imposed on all Jews wherever they resided a poll tax of 2 drachms.

However, before he could complete the task, Bassus died suddenly and the command was handed over to Flavius Silva. It was now his responsibility to capture the last outpost of Jewish resistance, Masada.

> Flavius Silva who, now seeing the whole country subjugated by the Roman arms, with the exception of one fortress still in revolt, concentrated all forces in the district and marched against it. This fortress was called Masada.[6]

Jonathan, the High Priest possibly in the second century BC, first fortified Masada, however Herod the Great erected the main buildings on the site. Scholars are divided whether this is Jonathan, the brother of Judas Maccabee (middle of the second century BC) or Alexander Jannaeus 176–103 BC who was known in Hebrew as Jonathan.

This is how Josephus describes the fortress:

> The report goes that Herod thus prepared this fortress as a refuge for himself suspecting a twofold danger; peril on the one hand from the Jewish people ... the greater and more serious from Cleopatra, queen of Egypt. She never concealed her intention but was ever importuning Antony urging him to slay Herod and praying him to confer on her the throne of Judaea.[7]

He tells of the spectacular palace Herod built there. It was constructed on the western ascent, beneath the walls of the citadel, inclined to its north side. The wall of the palace was high with four towers, one at each corner. The palace contained cloisters, baths and many other rooms all lavishly furnished and covered with mosaic floors.[8] The great plateau on the top of this rock cut fortress measured 600 metres (1,975 ft) north–south and 300 metres (975 ft) east–west at its widest point, is almost entirely circled by cliffs. Along part of the eastern side there is a 400 metre (1,250 ft) sheer drop, and from this side the only way to reach the top is by a precipitous winding single-lane path known from antiquity as the 'snake' path.

The ascent from the western side was much easier only being 75 metres (250 ft) from ground level to the summit but once again there was only one route to the top. The site was heavily fortified with a perimeter wall 1,300 metres (4,275 ft) long circumventing almost the entire length of the summit. The wall was about 5 metres (16 ft) high, strengthened by the addition of numerous towers. There were large supplies of arms in the fortress, Josephus says enough for 10,000 men although this is probably an exaggeration on his part, and large quantities of food and water. Herod had constructed huge cisterns and a system of dams and aqueducts to fill them during the rainy season. Therefore this site was a particularly difficult place to attack, for most of the year Masada was surrounded by parched wasteland of rock and sand. Any supplies would have to be hauled over many miles of difficult desert terrain, risking losses not only from sudden bandit attacks. This then was the prospect that faced the Roman legions sent to capture it.

The resistance was led by Eleazar b. Yair who came from an old revolutionary family that included the notorious Hezekiah the bandit chief responsible for terrorizing the neighbourhood of Galilee, who had carried out his raids as far as the Syrian frontier. They probably comprised of the remnants of Aristobulus' party, always strong in Galilee and who still looked for the succession of the sole male survivor of the family, Antigonus. Herod the Great was then military governor of Galilee and vigorously tackled the problem rounding up the bandits and killing them in 48–47 BC. Hezekiah's son was Judas, organiser of the tax revolt against Rome in AD 6 and a possible founder of the Zealot movement; his son Menahem was a prominent Zealot leader in Jerusalem in AD 66.

Accompanying Eleazar on this mountain fortress were 960 followers referred to by Josephus as *Sicarians*, although he also describes them in the text as Zealots. However, there seems to have been a spilt between the two groups, the Jerusalem group who established itself on Temple Mount under Eleazar b. Simon in November AD 66 (these were the men later absorbed by John of Gischala's group), and the Masada contingent, who had kept away from Jerusalem after they had been expelled that same year. After the death of Menahem by government forces, the leadership appears to have passed to his kinsman Eleazar b. Yair, who followed a strategy of rural banditry and guerrilla warfare.

It appears the group at Masada were one of the many that had dealings with Simon b. Giora during his campaigns in southern Judaea and Idumaea in AD 67–69. Josephus tells us that they had disagreed over strategy. Simon failed to persuade them to undertake anything other than raids around Masada, therefore they remained entrenched in their fortress supporting themselves by the raids they carried out, still intent on waging war against Rome.

The excavations carried out at Masada have demonstrated they lived in small family groups; many of the 110 rooms of the casement wall had been divided to create domestic units. There were also ritual baths and more importantly a synagogue which contained fragments of Holy text, one of which was singularly important for identifying the defenders of Masada, who would appear to have been politico-religious revolutionaries and not just the 'bandits' Josephus would have us believe they were.

The Romans certainly took the threat of insurgency seriously for any uprising would undermine the stability of the new Flavian regime, and could well spark other revolts in different parts of the empire. So in the winter of AD 72/3 or 73/4 a Roman force of approximately 15,000 men, comprising the X legion, auxiliaries, civilians and numerous Jewish slaves, responsible for carrying food and water, arrived at the foot of the fortress.

Silva had pacified and garrisoned the region ensuring the rebels were now confined to the fortress. He then established a blockade round it, and set to building eight camps for his troops and a wall of circumvallation over three miles in circumference. Two of the eight camps were vexillation camps, each one could accommodate half a legion, and these were built just behind the Roman wall opposite the two approaches to the fortress on both the east and the west. The other six camps were for the auxiliaries, two were military and could hold roughly 1,000 men each, the others were *quingenary* and could hold about 500 men. The auxiliary camps were sited to cover the main approaches, possible escape routes and in the case of one of them, to allow observation into Masada from above. In total the camps provided accommodation for about 9,000 men; slaves presumably were housed in temporary shelters.

The camps were organized into regular tent lines, one for each century of 80 men, with separate cells for each eight-man section.[9] The cells were formed of drystone walls with benches for sitting and sleeping, across the top of which, supported on poles, leather tents were spread. The wall of circumvallation that even went along the tops of vertical cliffs was nearly 2 metres (6 ft) thick, and was reinforced on the eastern side, where a possible breakout might occur, by 15 towers set at 70 to 90 metre (230–300 ft) intervals. Silva was determined there would be nothing left to chance, there was no way the Romans would take any risks the rebels might escape to continue the struggle elsewhere; for Rome this had to be the final battle for Judaea.

The only possible way to defeat the rebels would be to storm the citadel; a blockade would have been pointless as they had enough supplies to last for an indefinite period. To storm the fortress the Romans needed to employ an assault ramp, and there was only one place where this could be located, even so the prospect was daunting and would require consummate engineering skill.

Beyond the edge of the western gate was a ridge of high ground, which Josephus refers to as the 'white cliff' and here Silva ordered his men to build a huge ramp of earth and timber on top of it, raising the height by approximately 30 metres (100 ft). At the upper end of the ramp, close to the fortress walls the Romans constructed a level fighting platform, on to which they hauled their engines, which included a massive iron-plated tower almost 30 metres (100 ft) high filled with stone throwers and bolt shooters to rid the battlements of rebel defenders, and a huge ram which quickly smashed through a section of the wall.

The Zealots too had been busy and must surely have offered resistance to the Roman operations in typical guerrilla fashion. The excavations at Masada revealed huge stone boulders located in various casement rooms at strategic positions along the perimeter walls, evidence to demonstrate they were employing some defensive measures. Josephus does tell us, however, that while the Romans were battering down the wall the defenders were busy constructing a new wall behind it.

> The siccari, however, had already hastily built up another wall inside which was not likely to meet with a similar fate from the engines; for it was pliable and calculated to break the force of the impact.

Josephus then goes on to say how it was constructed,

> Great beams were laid lengthwise and contiguous and joined at the extremities; of these there were two parallel rows a walls breadth apart, and the intermediate space was filled with earth. Further to prevent the soil from dispersing as the mound rose, they clamped by other transverse beams, those laid longitudinally. The work thus presented to the enemy the appearance of masonry but the blows of the engines were weakened, battering upon yielding material, which as it settled down under the concussion, they merely served to solidify.[10]

Of course the new wall was vulnerable to fire and consequently Silva ordered his men to shoot volleys of fire-brands at the wall. Soon the fire took hold, although a change in the direction of the wind did at one point threaten to turn the flames back on to the siege engines. However, the wind changed direction yet again and the wall caught light. By the end of the day the second wall had been destroyed leaving a wide breach into the fortress. The following morning the Roman assault would begin, and that night the Roman watch was doubled to prevent anyone attempting to leave Masada by any exit.

However, the Zealots had contingency plans. The next morning Silva ordered the advance and the Romans stormed the fortress. On their arrival the following morning they found no rebels in the breach and no rebels in the compound beyond. In fact, all was quiet, the legionaries were perplexed and shouted hoping the enemy should show themselves. The only sign of life was when two women and five children emerged from a water channel where they had been hiding. They were the only survivors of the rebel community numbering 960 people.

One of the women told what had happened the night before and her account was entered in the official Roman log, which Josephus would most probably have consulted. There has been some doubt cast by scholars on the veracity of the story but it seems that there is little doubt that the basic factual record is correct.

It appears Eleazar persuaded his followers to enter into a suicide pact rather than allow themselves to fall into Roman hands. The men first killed their wives and children, and made a huge bonfire of their belongings. Then they drew lots and ten men were selected to kill their companions, each of whom lay down next to his wife and children and waited for their throat to be cut. Then the remaining ten drew lots and one was selected to kill the other nine before killing himself. This was the sight that greeted the Romans that morning, rows of bodies lying in their family groups.

Josephus gives a moving account of the speech that Eleazar delivered to his people the night of 15 April AD 73/4.

My loyal followers, long ago we resolved to serve neither the Romans nor anyone else but only God who alone is the true and righteous lord of men: now the time has come that bids us determination by our deeds. At such a time we must not disgrace ourselves: hitherto we have never submitted to slavery, even when it brought no danger with it; we must not chose slavery now and with it penalties that will mean the end of everything if we fall alive into the hands of the Romans. For we were the first of all to revolt and shall be the last to break off the struggle. And I think it is god who has given us this privilege that we can die nobly and as free men, unlike others who were unexpectedly defeated, in our case it is evident that day break will end our resistance, but we are free to choose an honourable death with our loved ones. This our enemies cannot prevent, however earnestly they may pray to take us alive; nor can we defeat them in battle.

Let our wives die un-abused, our children without knowledge of slavery: after that, let us do an ungrudging kindness, preserving our freedom as a glorious winding sheet. But first let our possessions and the whole fortress go up in flames: it will be a bitter blow to the Romans, that I know, to find our persons beyond their reach and nothing left for them to loot. One thing only let us spare our store of food; it will bear witness when we are dead to the fact that we perished, not through want but because, as we resolved at the beginning, we chose death rather than slavery.

If only we had all died before seeing the Sacred City utterly destroyed by enemy hands, the Holy Sanctuary so impiously uprooted! But since an honourable ambition deluded us into thinking that perhaps we should succeed in avenging her of her enemies, and now all hope has fled, abandoning us to our fate, let us at once choose death with honour and do the kindest thing we can for ourselves, our wives and children, while it is still possible to show ourselves any kindness. After all we were born to die, we, and those we brought into the world; this even the luckiest must face. But outrage, slavery and the sight of our wives led away to shame with our children – these are not evils to which man is subject by the laws of nature; men undergo them through their own cowardice if they have a chance to forestall them by death and will not take it. We are very proud of our courage, so we revolted against Rome: now in the final stages they have offered to spare our lives and we have turned the offer down. Is anyone too blind to see how furious they will be if they take us alive? Pity the young whose bodies are strong enough to survive prolonged torture; pity the not so young whose old frames would break under such ill usage. A man will see his wife violently carried off; he will hear the voice of his child crying, 'Father!' when his own hands are fettered. Come! While our hands are free and can hold a sword,

let them do a noble service! Let us die un-enslaved by our enemies, and leave this world
as free men in company with our wives and children.[11]

It seems apparent Josephus had no direct information about what happened at
Masada. Military activities were recorded; the account of the surviving women
was also recorded, so he tells us, but this may probably have circulated by word of
mouth, rather than actually written down. However, the organization of the Jews
and the exact nature of their resistance still remains a mystery. One prominent
Josephus scholar has made an observation on this by stating that Josephus in his
account: 'Took an unexpected step; with an act of imagination he put himself
among the defenders, and transformed that final scene into an extended dramatic
narrative'.[12]

Obviously, Josephus did not invent the incident at Masada, it seems what
he did do, however, was to create two very important speeches for Eleazar,
intended to inspire admiration for the man who uttered them. Eleazar and his
Zealot companions are made into virtual heroes, which would appear rather
strange considering his vehemence throughout the rest of his texts towards these
groups. One explanation is that he uses a well-contrived literary device when he
contrasts the Roman triumph with the Jewish episode at Masada that provides
a counterweight to the Roman victory. He allocates a prominent position in his
final book to the fate of Masada when he could have closed it with an account
of the end of the war proper.

However, the incident at Masada is not the end of his book, the *Jewish War*
concludes with the death of a persecutor; he gives a graphic account of the disease
which afflicted the Governor of Libya after he had executed approximately 3,000
wealthy Jews on a false charge of revolutionary activity and had others dragged
in chains to Rome.

Now contemplating the aftermath of the revolt he is tossed to and fro,
extending emotion in various directions. Along with his homeland he has for
a time lost his mental anchorage, and here it is shown in his writing. In this
way it continues to be an immediate product of pressing circumstances, and
to illuminate them through the strong responses expressed, and through its
weaknesses as history and literature.[13]

The war with Rome did continue, for others carried on the revolutionary ideology,
and the cause continued in other parts of the empire. Some Zealots made their way
to Alexandria in Egypt and attempted to build a base there but were handed over
to the Romans by the Jewish nobles. The reaction to their continued defiance even
under torture was to abolish the Jewish Temple of the Egyptian Jews at Onias.

In Cyrene there were also disturbances. Another Zealot fugitive, Jonathan,
led a group of poorer citizens into the desert promising to show them signs

and portents. The Jewish nobility denounced him also, and Rome despatched a military force to deal with them. Jonathan escaped but was later captured and taken in chains to Rome where he was tortured before being burnt alive.

Nevertheless Zealotism continued. There were further bouts of insurrection in AD 115–17 in the cities of the Diaspora, in Cyrene, Egypt and Cyprus until in AD 132–6 there was another rebellion in Palestine. This final revolt was connected with Simon Bar Kochba, whose name translates as Son of the Star, the new Jewish Messiah. The greatest Jewish sage of the time, the radical rabbi Akiva recognized and supported his claims. The rebels managed to win back the Holy city of Jerusalem, rebuilt its walls, appointed a new High Priest, and restored Temple ritual. They issued a variety of coins that proclaimed the Redemption of Israel. They were supported by volunteers and exiles now returned to Palestine from the Diaspora. The countryside was teeming with armed guerrilla fighters and once again the caves and desert fortresses were defended by Jewish freedom fighters. It took Rome four years and eight legions to crush this rebellion, and we have less information about the events than for the Jewish war. There was no Josephus to write an account, for he had died almost 20 years before in Rome, having served his Roman patrons with an account of their triumph over the Jews, and served history with one of the most complete accounts known from the ancient world.

15

Epilogue

They poured on to the streets sword in hand, cut down
without mercy all who came within reach, and burnt the houses of
any who took refuge indoors. (JW 6:403)

In 1970 excavations were being carried out in the Jewish quarter of the old city in Jerusalem when archaeologists uncovered the remains of a house dated to the fall of the city in AD 70. The site of the 'burnt house' is open to public viewing, and is impressive, vividly bringing to life the words of Josephus above concerning that tragic event.

At ground-floor level the building consisted of a small courtyard, five rooms and a ritual bath. The upper walls had collapsed and beneath the rubble was buried a layer of earth, ash, charred wood, soot, broken glass, potsherds, stone vessels and iron nails. Many of the objects had been broken before being scorched by fire. The plastered walls were blackened with soot, and scattered across the floor were coins, some from the period of the old procurators and some from the revolutionary period. If any further proof were needed of the violence that had taken place here then it was found; the remains of a human arm, with hand outstretched, as if grasping a step, was uncovered near the kitchen doorway.

Until the time of this discovery the only other major archaeological site of note relating to the struggle of the Jews against Rome was Masada. Excavations were undertaken here in the 1960s by Yadin when the site was re-discovered and the impact of Josephus' account of the heroic last stand of the Jews against their enemies re-awakened a nationalistic response from the newly formed state of Israel. The nationalistic fervour created was so intense all Israeli soldiers swore their oath of allegiance on the top of this rock fortress and the words 'Masada shall not fall again' became a watchword for a new generation of Jews.

Certainly the most visually dramatic material results from the excavations carried out by Yadin in 1963/5. The site is indeed impressive; today a cable car takes you to the summit, but for the more energetic the old route via the 'snake path' is an alternative ascent. From the top the remains of the Roman camps are clearly visible, and are by far the best preserved of any Roman camps anywhere in Europe. The remaining buildings on the site itself including the upper and lower palaces are also well preserved.

However, the archaeological record attesting to the final events here, the mass suicide of over 900 people, is disappointing for there was little trace of any human skeletal remains whatsoever. That is not to say they may not have been buried somewhere in the desert vicinity of the fortress, but if this is the case then only a chance find will confirm it. Despite the fact no skeletons were discovered there was proof, however, of extensive fire and destruction. Some rooms remained undamaged while in others, pieces of furniture, nails and metal were found to be all fire damaged, which may reflect the evidence supplied by Josephus of the last actions of the Zealots who made haste to assemble all their goods in one place and set fire to them.

Among the other buildings on the site was a house of study, indicating that the defenders of Masada were religious and not just bandit revolutionaries that Josephus so often calls them. The house of study (*Bet Midras*) contained stone benches that were sited along the walls framing a central hall indicating the study house could also have been used as a meeting place; somewhere no doubt where the strategy to foil the Roman assault was debated. The priests and Levites whose status was preserved and recognized at Masada conducted religious services. The coupons for their rations are marked *ma'asar kohen* (priest's tithe), in acknowledgement of the commandment of tithing. Other ostraka (potsherds) had letters inscribed on them, T (for *truma* gift offering) or *tevel* (untithed produce). Special rations were also allocated for ritual purposes as evidenced by appropriate inscriptions on the jars *kodesh* (holy) *ksherin* (clean for the purposes of holiness). The Zealots had brought Bible scrolls with them to Masada and fragments of these were also found from the books of Genesis, Leviticus, Deuteronomy, Ezechial and Psalms. Their sacred writings even included some of the apocryphal works like Ben Sirach and Jubilees.

The Messianic, and some would say revolutionary, sect that were established at Qumran on the shores of the Dead Sea, the Essenes, also had members amongst the refugees at Masada and they also brought their sectarian literature such as the *Song of the Sabbath Sacrifices*. It is clear from the evidence retrieved men of different sects and beliefs found themselves united together on this rocky fortress in the desert for one last attempt to be free from their Roman masters.

Perhaps the most exciting of all the finds, although perhaps amongst the smallest, was a piece of ostrakon. Near the inner gate leading to the northern complex were found ten small ostraka with a name or nick-name scratched on to them, 'the bakers son', 'the man from the valley', 'Joab' etc. But one piece of ostrakon bore the name Beniar (Ben Yair), could this be the leader Eleazar? And the remaining pieces bear the names of the ten men chosen by lot to despatch their comrades?

More recent excavations at Masada undertaken in 1996 have yielded a variety of interesting finds that told something of the everyday life of the revolutionaries who lived and died here, such items as Italian glass vessels and Nabatean table-ware. Amongst the material unearthed were a mass of small pebbles piled in a heap near the northern end, no doubt these had been used as slingshot against the Roman forces assembled below. There is no more compelling site than Masada and perhaps it is here that one can truly appreciate the struggle of the Jews against the might of Rome.

However, there is still a great deal we do not know about the war, and research continues both historically and archaeologically to understand and elucidate the truth from the works of Josephus. In recent years many of the sites associated with the rebellion in Galilee have also come under scrutiny. It would appear from the time of Herod the Great up to the period of the revolt Jews in Galilee were no longer purchasing one particular type of ceramic, red slip bowl commonly known as eastern *sigillata*, brightly coloured fancy table vessels. Their acquisition performed a convenient communicative role as a manifestation of foreign and specifically Roman control. It has been argued that this lack of material evidence demonstrates that Galilean Jews deliberately rejected them in a 'simple political statement of solidarity and affinity with a traditional simple unadorned Jewish lifestyle'.[1] Does this mean that Galilee was a hotbed of dissent right from start, or that the people of Galilee were more traditional than their city brethren? Clearly this is a topic that will be continually debated by scholars.

Gamala was a city that had suffered both siege and battle and is described by Josephus in some detail. Excavations were carried out here from 1976–89 and in 1995 archaeologists attempted to assess the events that took place here during the revolt 'as reported by Josephus and filtered through the archaeological evidence'.[2] With the exception of Jotapata Gamala is one of the few examples of a battle site of the first century AD throughout the Roman Empire left as it was abandoned. Since the site was never resettled it provided for the archaeologist an unparalleled glimpse of Jewish life in the last decades of the Second Temple period.

> The city which nature had rendered so impregnable, Josephus had fortified with walls and secured still further by mines and trenches. Its occupants felt greater confidence in the nature of their site than did those of Jotapata, though far inferior to them in the number of combatants; indeed such trust they had in their position that they would admit no more.[3]

Josephus says the city was so well fortified it attracted many refugees from the rebellion as well as people from the local community and neighbouring towns, who felt secure behind its walls. Two areas in the city were excavated and supplied evidence for occupation by such refugees; for example in the western quarters even the synagogue had been converted to a dwelling area. Remains were also uncovered of meagre fireplaces, cooking utensils, storage jars; all were uncovered beneath a quantity of ballista balls used by the Romans to smash the place down.

The suicide at Masada is paralleled in the writings of Josephus by his account of the suicide at Gamala, when:

> Despairing of their lives and hemmed in on every side, multitudes plunged headlong with their wives and children into the ravine which had been excavated to a vast depth beneath the citadel. Indeed the rage of the Romans was thus made to appear milder than the fanatic self immolation of the vanquished, four thousand only being slain by the former, while those who flung themselves over the cliff were found to exceed five thousand.[4]

However, one scholar has taken a pragmatic approach to disproving the suicide story: for as already noted, the only place along the ridge where there is a vertical cliff high enough for someone falling off it to die with any reasonable certainty, can only be reached with some difficulty. Even in antiquity when the ridge may have been much larger it would still only have accommodated around 500 people. The second point is that in the heat of battle it would hardy have been likely they would have had time to rally and decide on mass suicide. It would seem more feasible that the remaining defenders and townspeople were trying to flee down the steep northern slope and were trampled underfoot in the ensuing panic.

Josephus may well have witnessed the event from the nearby ridge at Deir Qaruh and perhaps to him it may have looked like mass suicide. However, the physical evidence suggests not. During the 14 years of excavations carried out on this site, as with Masada no human skeleton has been found. This may of course reflect the Jewish religious command for burial of the dead. The Romans may well have allowed the Jews to return to bury the bodies while at the same time doing them a service by way of removing a health hazard. If so the dead were most probably interred in a mass grave somewhere in the vicinity and as with Masada their discovery will only come about by chance. The recent discovery of a mass burial in a cistern at Jotapata seems to confirm this theory.

Jotapata was the site of the second bloodiest battle after the battle of Jerusalem, and the third longest siege after Jerusalem and Masada and of course the battle in which Josephus played a key role as commander of the defending forces. Examination of the site revealed two phases of fortification one from the Hellenistic period and one during the early Roman period. The excavations revealed the hastily constructed fortifications which followed the line of topography dated to the first century AD and probably identifiable with the efforts described by Josephus.

During the 1999 excavation season three areas of the Roman wall circuit were uncovered, one of which revealed the remains of a private dwelling. In another area three casements were excavated all surviving to their foundations. In the westernmost room a short narrow shaft was discovered which led to a narrow tunnel with a gabled roof that opened into three rock cut chambers, which clearly served as hideouts. Other evidence of the battle was found, apart from arrowheads and ballistas; the remains of earthworks were also located.

> It was decided to erect earthworks against the accessible portion of the wall, whereupon the whole army was sent out to procure the necessary materials. The mountain forests surrounding the town were stripped, and besides timber, enormous masses of stones were collected.[5]

The layers of stony soil confirmed this account by Josephus and furthermore mortar was uncovered that the Romans had used to build the ramp.

Once again the issue of suicide raises its head. Besides this site, only three other battle sites have been excavated, Masada, Gamala and Jerusalem and only very few skeletal remains have been found. However, the finds at Jotapata have been more encouraging. There were some part-burnt human bones found in the weight pit of the cave that contained the oil press. At the bottom of a cistern in one field was a burial chamber containing the remains of two adults and a child, and further bones were found in the upper level of a cistern in another field.

During the 1999 excavations in the northern part of the same field, a large cistern was uncovered revealing many human bones and skulls. Analysis showed the remains belonged to about 20 different people, 12 adults including four females and eight children under 18 years of age. Other finds include pottery from the first century AD and ballista stones. Further excavations here may well reveal more skeletal remains. The evidence suggests the Romans allowed the inhabitants of Jotapata to return and bury their dead. However, according to the excavators, the numbers of the dead given by Josephus may have been exaggerated. Some human skeletal remains were found on the site of the northern palace at Masada and some complete skeletons in a cave below the cliff. In Jerusalem only the remains of an arm from the Burnt House have so far been discovered, and at Gamala one human jaw-bone. The story of Jotapata is one of the most detailed in the whole *War* saga and these excavations have succeeded in proving many aspects of Josephus narrative to be correct.

However, the most enduring monument to the Jewish war still stands today in Rome, the remaining one of three Arches of Titus, representing of course the Roman view, and which marked out the processional route taken by the triumph. The first arch was constructed in AD 79–81, and the Arch of Titus in the Circus

Maximus in AD 81, the surviving arch was completed after his death in AD 81. The reliefs on the arch show the spoils taken from the Temple, processing through the streets to their final resting place in the Temple of Peace.

What is significant about the arch completed in AD 81 was its exceptional prominence, a visible reminder to over 100,000 people of the capture of Jerusalem. Part of the inscription reveals a blatantly false claim:

> on the instructions and advice of his father [Vespasian], and under his auspices he subdued the race of the Jews and destroyed the city of Jerusalem, which by all generals, kings or races previous to himself had either been attacked in vain or not even attempted at all.[6]

Josephus' book *Jewish War* had already been written and had recorded the fact Jerusalem had been captured by the Roman general Pompey in 63 BC and again by Sosius in 37 BC; indeed Sosius had built a temple in honour of his achievement near the Theatre of Marcellus. So it is incomprehensible the Romans would not have been aware of their previous history.

Titus died not long after the inscription was put in place. The remaining surviving arch was erected after his death so it could be viewed as a commemorative arch. The arch lies along the route to the Colosseum the great amphitheatre that excites and attracts millions of visitors from every corner of the world, and the greatest of all the monuments erected by the Flavians.

A recent inscription find from the amphitheatre shows the two monuments are even more closely connected to the Jewish war than was previously thought. It appears the construction of the Colosseum was paid for from the 'spoils of war', there is no reference to Judaea but there had been no other war with which the Flavians were involved, so it can be accepted the reference is to the Jewish war.[7] It is poignant to contemplate the feelings and thoughts of those Jewish prisoners who found themselves forced into the arena to compete in the bloody spectacles there, it is almost as if the Jewish state had financed their deaths.

The archaeological record is far from complete and who knows what future discoveries await archaeologists and researchers; indeed the story is far from over concerning events in Judaea in the first century AD.

Notes

1   Faulkner, N. (2002) *Apocalypse: The Great Jewish Revolt against Rome*. 383.
2   Berlin, A. and Overman J. (eds)(2002) *The First Jewish Revolt* Introduction. They refer to him as 'this famous and provocative historian'.
3   ibid. 'As eyewitness to many events of the revolt he is therefore an invaluable historical source. He was able to do this because he was a capitulator working with the Roman forces.'
4   Goodman, M. (1987) *The Ruling Class of Judaea*, Schwartz, S. (1990) *Josephus and Judaean Politics*.
5   Rajak, T. (2000) *Josephus*; McLaren, J.S. (1998) *Turbulent Times?: Josephus and Scholarship in Judaea in the First Century* CE.
6   Goodman (1987).

Notes Chapter 1.

1   1 Maccabees 27.
2   Josephus *JW* 1:402–28.
3   Avi-Yonah, M. (2001) *A History of Israel and the Holy Land* 149.
4   Strabo *Geography* XVII 3.25 (840).
5   Tacitus *Histories* 1.11.
6   Schürer, E. (rev. 1973) *History of the Jewish People in the age of Jesus Christ* Vol. I Chapter 17.
7   Tacitus *Histories* 5.9.
8   ibid 5:5.
9   Rajak 106.

Notes Chapter 2.

1   *Life* 8.
2   *Life* 12.
3   *Life* 23.
4   *Life* 29.
5   For further information on the mathematical information concerning the Josephus count, and to play the number game visit www.cut-the-knot-org/rec/flavius
6   Suetonius 'Vespasian', *The Twelve Caesars* 5. Abot de-R. Nathan 4, 5

7   *Life* 426–7.
8   Roth, C. (1959) Introduction *The Jewish War*.
9   *Life* 429–30.
10 Eusebius *Ecclesiastical History and Martyres of Palestine* iii, 9.
11 *JA* 20: 262.
12 Schürer 49.
13 Schalit, A. (1965) 'Evidence of an aramaic source in Josephus' Antiquities of the Jews'. *ASTI.* 4 163–88.
14 For a full list of other non-Biblical source material used by Josephus see Schürer 49, ft 13.
15 For a more favourable view of Josephus' use of Nicolaus of Damascus' work see Prof. Ben Zion Wacholder, 'Josephus and Nicolaus of Damascus' in Feldman and Hata (eds) (1989) *Josephus the Bible and History*.
16 Thackery, H. St J. (1967) *Josephus the Man and the Historian* 37.
17 *Against Apion* i.9.40.
18 *Antiquities* 10.10.4.
19 Daniel 2:44.
20 For example, Rajak esp. 220–1.
21 ibid 221.
22 For a good discussion of the way in which Josephus manipulates the events on Masada see Broshi, M. (1982) 'The credibility of Josephus'. *JJS* Vol. 33 379.
23 *JW* 1.15.
24 Goodman (1987).

Notes Chapter 3.

1   Bilde, P. (1979) 'The causes of the Jewish War according to Josephus'. *JSJ* Vol. X. No. 2.
2   Goodman, Rappaport, Smallwood.
3   *JW* 4:386–8.
4   *JW* 2:457–90.
5   Not all decisions made by Rome were insensitive to Judaea, for example the emperor Claudius' appointment of Agrippa I as king in AD 41 was designed to placate Jewish feelings after the disastrous episode with Caligula.
6   Smallwood, E.M. (1981) *The Jews under Roman Rule* 284.
7   Bilde *op. cit.*
8   Smallwood Ch. 11.
9   See Sorek, S.M. (2002) 'Render unto Caesar, Pilate and the Temple funds'. *Eras Online Journal*. Monash University School of Historical Studies. Edition 4. December.
10 Philo *Legatio*.
11 ibid.
12 Kindler, A. (1974) *Coins of the Land of Israel*.
13 Smallwood 167.
14 The 'Testimonium Flavianum' summary of the life of Christ (*AJ* 18:63–4) is a topic of controversy. For further information on this see Feldman, Loeb ed. *Antiquities* 1985.

15   Tacitus *Histories* 5.10.
16   Millar, F. (1977) *The Emperor in The Roman World.*
17   *JW* 2:220.
18   Gabba, E. (1999) 'The social, economic and political history of Palestine 63 BCE-CE 70' in *The Cambridge History of Judaism Vol. 3 The Early Roman Period* 141
19   Tacitus *Annals* 12.54.
20   The account of Felix that appears in Acts is taken from an account written by the accusers of St Paul to prejudice the procurator against the man who they considered a disruptive element.
21   *JW* 2:26ff.
22   Tacitus *Histories.* 5.10.

Notes Chapter 4.

1   Goodman, M. (2006) *Rome and Jerusalem: The Clash of Ancient Civilisations* 169ff.
 2   Ezekiel 18.2.
 3   Smallwood 293.
 4   Goodman (1987) 20.
 5   Bilde 193.
 6   *JA* 18:10.
 7   *JA* 18:25.
 8   Daniel 2:44.
 9   *JW* 4:225.
10   Goodman (1987) 201; Horsley, R.A. (1996) 'Zealots, the origin, relationship and importance in the Jewish revolt'. *Novum Testamentum* XXVIII. 2.
11   Roth, C. (1959) 'The Zealots in the war of 66–73 AD'. *JSS* IV (iv). Numbers 25.2.
12   Mishnah *Peser* 10.9–13.
13   *JA* 18:10.
14   Smallwood 155.

Notes Chapter 5.

1   See Sorek (2002).
 2   Goodman (1987) 171.
 3   *JW* 2:295.
 4   *JW* 2:311.
 5   *JW* 2:397–9.
 6   Confirmed by Talmud.
 7   *JW* 2:426–7.
 8   *JW* 2:484–60.
 9   *JW* 2:457–80.

Notes Chapter 6.

1 *JW* 2:525–6.
2 *JW* 2:531.
3 *JW* 2:523. See also Goodman (2006).
4 *JA* 2:160.
5 *JW* 2:550.
6 *JW* 2:556.
7 ibid.
8 A full account is given by Roth, C. (1964) *JSemJ* ix 295–319.
9 Smallwood 299.
10 See Faulkner (2002) 180.
11 Kindler.

Notes Chapter 7.

1 See Rajak, T. (1973) 'Justus of Tiberias' *CQ* 23 364–68.
2 Horsley (1993) in particular makes this point in *Jesus and the Spiral of Violence: Popular Jewish Resistance in Roman Palestine* Ch. 4.
3 Rajak (2000) 147–9.
4 ibid 167. There are some instances where the account in *War* seems more reliable, notably 2:565 compared with *Life* 28. According to her, with regard to some aspects of the narrative, *Vita* [Life] gives flesh to the bones of *BJ* [War].
5 *Life* 22.
6 Goodman (1987) 158–9.
7 ibid.
8 Rajak (2000) 168.
9 Vermes, G. (1983) *Jesus the Jew* Ch. 2, 44.
10 Schwartz, S. 'Josephus in Galilee: rural patronage and social breakdown', in Parente, F. and Sievers J. (eds) (1994) *Josephus and the History of the Graeco-Roman Period.* 290–308. It should be noted that this view is diametrically opposed to Goodman's hypothesis.
11 Rajak (2000)(159) says that Josephus made an incorrect statement when he said Sepphoris was eager for war. Smallwood (302) says Sepphoris had declared for the rebels despite being in Roman hands.
12 *JW* 3:129. According to Josephus the priests had been bribed by John.
13 *Life* 67ff.
14 *JW* 2:607.
15 *Life* 44–5.
16 See Rappaport, U. (1982) 'John of Gischala, from Galilee to Jerusalem'. *JJS* 33 479–93. The same assertions cannot be made for the other notable Galilean leader Simon b. Gioras; although Goodman makes the claim for him being of noble lineage, this is strongly criticised by Geiger in his review of Goodman's book (1987) see *JRA* 2 (1989) 291–4.
17 ibid.

18 Goodman (1987) 165 and 182–5. This is inferred from John's association with Simon b. Gamaliel (*Life* 192, 195).

19 Rajak (2000) 162ff.

20 ibid 160.

21 Schwartz, S. (1994) 'Josephus in Galilee' 290–308.

22 Goodman (1987) 51–75.

23 See also Applebaum, S. 'The struggle for soil and the revolt of 66–73CE' in Feldman and Hata (eds) *Josephus, the Bible and History* 237ff.

24 ibid.

25 On absentee landlords see *New Testament* Matthew 21: 33–4, and *Midrash* Lamentations Rabbah II.5.

26 *Life* 35ff.

27 Horsley Ch. 4.

28 *War* 2:31–6:320–4.

29 For an interesting discussion on the Jewish response to the power of Rome see B. D. Shaw, 'Josephus: Power and responses to it'. *Athenaeum* 83 1995.

Notes Chapter 8.

1 *JW* 3:138.

2 In Polybius *Histories*.

3 *JW* 3:231–3.

4 *Life* 35ff.

5 ibid.

6 *JW* 3:264.

7 *JW* 3:331.

8 *JW* 3:339–403.

9 ('Vesp.' 5, 6). This is also to be found in Tacitus *Histories* ii, 78, 3.

10 Rajak (2000) 167–72.

11 *JW* 3:295.

Notes Chapter 9.

1 *JW* 3:469–70.

2 *JW* 2:236 and 243ff.

3 *JW* 4:4–8.

4 *JW* 4:36.

5 *JW* 4:72–81.

6 Stern, M. (1982) 'The Suicide of Eleazar ben Yair and his men at Marada, and the Fourth Philosophy.

7 Syon, D. (2002) 'Gamala: City of Refuge' in Berlin and Overman (eds) *The First Jewish Revolt: Archaeology, History and Ideology.*

8   ibid 150.
9   *JW* 4:92.
10 *JW* 4:115.
11 *JW* 3:425–34.

Notes Chapter 10.

1   *JW* 4:125.
2   *JW* 4:159.
3   Ananus' impassioned speech can be found in *JW* 4:162–8.
4   *JW* 4:182–8.
5   *JW* 4:214.
6   *JW* 4:224.
7   *JW* 4:285.
8   *JW* 4:406.
9   Faulkner 286.
10 *JW* 4:401.
11 *JW* 4:523.
12 Tacitus *Histories* 5.12, 3–4
13 Goodman (1987) 178
14 *JW* 6:421.
15 Goodman (1987) 180.

Notes Chapter 11.

1   Dio Cassius *Histories* lxiii 19.
2   Qualis artifex pereo Suetonius *Nero* 49.
3   Tacitus *Histories* 1:27.
4   Suetonius 'Otho' 12.
5   *JW* 5:128ff.
6   Suetonius 'Vitellius' 10.
7   ibid.
8   Tacitus *Histories* 111 67–74.
9   ibid 79–85.
10 *JW* 4:592–8.
11 *JW* 4:592–604.
12 Goodman (1987) 180–1.

Notes Chapter 12.

1   Tacitus *Histories* 5.23.
2   *JW* 5:47–9.

3   *JW* 5:66.
4   *JW* 5:71.
5   *JW* 5:79–80.
6   *JW* 5:100.
7   *JW* 5:103ff.
8   *JW* 5:375.
9   *JW* 5:277.
10 *JW* 5:280.
11 *JW* 5:350.
12 *JW* 5:362.
13 *JW* 5:470–2.
14 *JW* 5:475.

Notes Chapter 13.

1   *JW* 5:531.
2   *JW* 6:9–14.
3   *JW* 6:16–17.
4   *JW* 6:86–7.
5   *JW* 6:97.
6   Known as *tmaid*, the daily sacrifice of lamb.
7   *JW* 6:1421–7.
8   *JW* 6:181–3.
9   From the *Chronicle of Sulpicius Severus* 5th century AD.
10 Rives, J. (2005) 'Flavian policy and the Jerusalem Temple' in Edmondson, Mason and Rives (eds) *Flavius Josephus and Flavian Rome* 147–66.
11 *JW* 6:271.
12 See Sorek, S.M. (2000) *Vows of Valuations* Postgraduate Journal Dept. of Classics. University of Cork Edition 2.
13 *JW* 6:352.
14 Goodman (1987) 200–1.
15 *JW* 6:403.
16 See Magness, J. (2002) 'In the footsteps of the 10th legion' in Berlin and Overman *The First Jewish Revolt* 190–1.

Notes Chapter 14.

1   *Life* 417–8.
2   *JW* 7:143–5.
3   *JW* 7:156–7.
4   Chapman, H.H. (2005) 'Spectacle in Josephus' Jewish War' in Edmondson, Mason and Rives (eds) *Flavius Josephus and Flavian Rome* 302.

5 *JW* 7:201–4.

6 *JW* 7:252.

7 *JW* 7:301.

8 See Yadin, Y. (1966) *Masada Herod's Fortress and the Zealots Last Stand.*

9 Known as *conturbernium.*

10 *JW* 7:311–12.

11 *JW* 7:385–8. Free trans. Sorek.

12 Rajak (2002) 220.

13 ibid 222.

Notes Chapter 15.

1 Berlin, A. (2002) 'Romanization and anti-Romanization in pre-Revolt Galilee' in Berlin and Overman (eds) *The First Jewish Revolt* 57–73.

2 Syon, D. ibid 134–55.

3 *JW* 4:10.

4 *JW* 4:79–80. See Aviam, M. (2002) 'Yodefat: The archaeology of the first battle' in Berlin and Overman (eds) *The First Jewish Revolt* 131.

5 *JW* 3:163–5.

6 *CIL* 6.944 *ILS* 264.

7 *CIL* 6 40454a *AE* 1995 111b.

Bibliography

PRIMARY SOURCES: EDITIONS & TRANSLATIONS CITED

BIBLICAL LITERATURE

Friberg Greek New Testament. Bible, New Revised Standard Version: New International Bible, all on *Bibleworks* CD Rom vv 4.0. Eds. Bushell, M. S. and Tan, M. D. (Big Fork, MS, 1992–1999).

Apocrypha. New Revised Standard Version (Cambridge: Cambridge University Press 1989).

RABBINIC LITERATURE

Babylonian Talmud. Soncino edn, Hebrew/English (Judaic Classics Library: CD Rom version 1996).

Mishnah. *The Mishnah Upon which the Palestinian Talmud Rests.* Trans. Lowe, W. H. (Cambridge: Cambridge University Press 1883).

Tosefta. Ed. Lieberman, S., 2nd edn (New York: Jewish Theological Seminary 1992).

GRAECO-ROMAN ANCIENT LITERATURE

Dio Cassius (1954) *Histories.* Trans. Long (London: Harvard University Press).

Eusebius (1954) *Ecclesiastical History and Martyrs of Palestine.* Trans. Lawlor Vol. 1 (London:*SPCK*).

Josephus (1997) *Antiquitates Judaicae, Bellum Judaicum, Vita, Contra Apionem.* Trans. Thackery, H. St.J. (London: Harvard University Press).

Philo (1991) *Works.* Trans. Coulson, F. H. (London: Harvard University Press).

Strabo (1959–69) *Geography* (London: Heinemann).

Suetonius (1989) *The Twelve Caesars* (Penguin: Harmondsworth).

Tacitus (1990) *Histories, Annals of Imperial Rome* (London: Harvard University Press).

SECONDARY SOURCES

Applebaum, S. (1975) 'The struggle for soil and the revolt of 66–73CE'. *Grets Israel* 12 125–8.

Avi-Yonah, M. (2001) *A History of Israel and the Holy Land* (London: Continuum) 149.

Avigad, N. (1980) *Discovering Jerusalem* (New York: Nelson Publishers).

Aviam, M. (2002) 'Yodefat: archaeology of the first battle' in Berlin, A. and Overman J. (eds) *The First Jewish Revolt* (London: Routledge). 121–33.

Berlin, A. (2002) 'Romanization and Anti-Romanization in pre-revolt Galilee' in Berlin, A. and Overman, J. (eds) *The First Jewish Revolt* (London: Routledge) 57–73.

Berlin, A. and Overman, J. (eds) (2002) *The First Jewish Revolt* (London: Routledge).

Bilde, P. (1979) 'The causes of the Jewish War according to Josephus'. *JSJ* Vol X. No 2.

Bond, H. (1998) *Pontius Pilate in History and Interpretation* (Cambridge: Cambridge University Press).

Broshi, M. (1982) 'The credibility of Josephus'. *JJS* Vol 33, 379.

Chapman, H. H. (2005) 'Spectacle in Josephus' Jewish War' in Edmondson, J., Mason. S. and Rives, J. (eds) *Flavius Josephus and Flavian Rome* (Oxford: Oxford University Press) 302.

Donaldson, T. (1990) 'Rural bandits, city mobs and Zealots'. *Journal of Jewish Studies* 31, 18–36.

Faulkner, N. (2002) *Apocalypse: The Great Jewish Revolt against Rome* (Stroud: Tempus).

Feldman, L.H. and Hata, G. (eds)(1989) *Josephus, the Bible and History* (USA: Wayne State University Press).

Gabba, E. (1999) 'The social, economic and political history of Palestine 63 BCE–CE 70' in *The Cambridge History of Judaism: Vol. 3 The Early Roman Period* (Cambridge: Cambridge University Press) 141.

Goodman, M. (1987) *The Ruling Class of Judaea* (Cambridge: Cambridge University Press).

Goodman, M. (2006) *Rome and Jerusalem: The Clash of Ancient Civilizations* (London: Penguin).

Gutman, S. and Shanks, H. (1979) 'Gamala: Masada of the North'. *Biblical Archaeology Review* 5.1, 12–27.

Horbury, W., Davies, W. D. and Sturdy, J. (eds) *Cambridge History of Judaism Vol. 3 The Early Roman Period* (Cambridge: Cambridge University Press).

Horsley, R. A. (1993) *Jesus and the Spiral of Violence: Popular Jewish Resistance in Roman Palestine* Ch.4, Augsburg, MN: Augsburg Fortress.

Horsley, R. A. (1996) 'Zealots, the origin, relationship and importance in the Jewish revolt'. *Novum Testamentum* XXVIII.2.

Kindler, A. (1974) *Coins of the Land of Israel* (Jerusalem: Keter).

McLaren, J.S. (1991) *Power and Politics in Palestine: The Jews and the Governing of their Land 100* BC–AD *70* (Sheffield: JSOT).

McLaren, J.S. (1998) *Turbulent Times?: Josephus and Scholarship in Judaea in the First Century* CE (Sheffield: Sheffield Academic Press).

Magness, J. (2002) 'In the footsteps of the 10th legion' in Berlin, A. M. and Overman, J. A. *The First Jewish Revolt* (London: Routledge) 190–1.

Millar, F. (1977) *The Emperor in The Roman World* (London: Duckworth).

Parente, F. and Sievers J. (eds) (1994) *Josephus and the History of the Graeco-Roman Period* (Leiden: Brill).

Rajak, T. (1973)'Justus of Tiberias'. *CQ* 23 364–68.

Rajak, T. (rep. 2002) *Josephus* (London: Duckworth).

Rappaport, U. (1982) 'John of Gischala – from Galilee to Jerusalem'. *JJS* 33 479–93.

Rappaport, U. (1992) 'How Anti Roman was the Galilee?' in Levine, L. (ed.) *The Galilee in Late Antiquity* Ch. 3 (New York: Jewish Theological Seminary).

Rhoads, D. M. (1976) *Israel in Revolution 6–74* CE (Philadelphia, PA: Fortress).

Rives, J. (2005) 'Flavian policy and the Jerusalem Temple' in Edmondson, J., Mason. S. and Rives, J. (eds) *Flavius Josephus and Flavian Rome* (Oxford: Oxford University Press), 147–66.

Roth, C. (1959) 'The Zealots in the war of 66–73AD' *JSS* IV (iv)11.

Roth, C. (1959) 'Introduction' *The Jewish War* (Harmondsworth: Penguin). Trans. Wilkinson.

Schalit, A. (1965) 'Evidence of an aramaic source in Josephus' Antiquities of the Jews'. *ASTI*, 4, 163–88.

Schürer, E. (rev. 1973) *History of the Jewish People in the Age of Jesus Christ* (Edinburgh: T & T Clark).

Schwarz, S. (1990) *Josephus and Judaean Politics* (Leiden: Brill).

Schwarz, S. (1994) 'Josephus in Galilee: Rural patronage and social breakdown' in E. Paronte and J. Sievers (eds) *Josephus and the History of the Graeco-Roman Period* (Leiden: Brill).

Shaw, B. D. (1995) 'Josephus: Power and responses to it' *Athenaeum* 83, 357–90.

Smallwood, E. M. (1981) *The Jews under Roman Rule* (Lieden: Brill) Chapter 11.

Sorek, S. M. (2000) *Vows of Valuations,* Postgraduate Journal Dept. of Classics. University of Cork, Edition 2.

Sorek, S. M. (2002) 'Render unto Caesar, Pilate and the Temple funds'. *Eras Online Journal,* Monash University School of Historical Studies, Edition 4, December.

Stern, M. (1982) 'The suicide of Eleazar ben Yair and his men at Masada and the Fourth Philosophy'. *Zion* 47 367–79 (HEB).

Syon, D. (2002) 'Gamala: City of Refuge' in Berlin, A. M. and Overman, J. A.
  (eds) *The First Jewish Revolt: Archaeology, History and Ideology* (New York:
  Routledge) 139–51.
Thackery, H. St John (1967) *Josephus the Man and the Historian* (New York:
  KTAV Publishing House).
Vermes, G. (1983) *Jesus the Jew* (Augsberg, MN: Augsburg Fortress).
Wacholder, Ben Zion (1989) 'Josephus and Nicolaus of Damascus' in Feldman,
  L. and Hata, G. (eds) (1989) *Josephus the Bible and History* (Leiden: Brill).
Yadin, Y. (1966) *Masada Herod's Fortress and the Zealots Last Stand* (London:
  Weidenfeld and Nicholson).

Index